DINNER

UNCOMPLICATED

CLAIRE TANSEY

DINNER
UNCOMPLICATED

Fixing a delicious meal every night of the week

PAGE TWO
BOOKS

Copyright © 2020 by Claire Tansey

Cataloguing in publication information is available from Library and Archives Canada.
ISBN 978-1-989603-39-0 (paperback)
ISBN 978-1-989603-74-1 (ebook)

Page Two
www.pagetwo.com

Edited by Katie Dupuis
Copyedited by Melissa Edwards
Proofread by Alison Strobel

Design by Peter Cocking
Photography by Suech and Beck
Food styled by Lindsay Guscott
Props styled by Emily Howes
Author's wardrobe by Miik

Printed and bound in Canada by Friesens
Distributed in Canada by Raincoast Books
Distributed in the US and internationally by
Publishers Group West, a division of Ingram

20 21 22 23 24   5 4 3 2 1

clairetansey.com

BULK ORDERS

If you're interested in bulk purchases of this book, please contact:

info@clairetansey.com

We offer a significant discount on bulk orders and would be happy to discuss options.

To everyone who makes dinner,
especially Michael, who makes it for me.

And to Thomas, who always says thank you.

And to whisky, for being great.

CONTENTS

What's for Dinner?

LET'S CALL IT a Wednesday, mid-afternoon. Lunch is a distant memory and you're starting to feel a bit peckish. Just then, your phone buzzes. It's your partner, parent, roommate or child, asking, "What's for dinner?" It's a watershed moment: You either send back a quick reply, high-five yourself and move on with your afternoon, or you tumble onto the floor, head in hands, wailing, "Why do we have to eat every single day?!"

I've been there—both the high-five and the meltdown—and frankly I'm tired of the latter; I want the high-five a lot more often. I love eating dinner with my family, and I want the whole process to be joyful instead of stressful. That's why I wrote this book. My first book, *Uncomplicated*, was all about sharing the recipes that prove cooking doesn't have to be difficult to be delicious. I wanted this book to be an even more practical guide to getting dinner on the table.

The rewards of having a home-cooked dinner are tremendous. It's the single best way to make a dramatic change in your life. What other little lifestyle change improves physical and mental health, plus the health of your finances, your family and our planet all at the same time? That's a heck of an impact from a plate of pasta (or a bowl of chili or an amazing burger or...).

But best of all, for me, having a daily dinner ritual brings more happiness into my life. When I eat with the people I love (whether I do the cooking or not!), I feel better, no matter what the world threw at me that day—and they feel better too!

Of course the trouble is pulling it all off. As much as we'd love to get a from-scratch meal on the table most nights of the week, it's a tall order. We're short on time, long on hunger and out of ideas.

The most common complaint I hear from my readers, students, friends and neighbours is that they don't have time. We're busy, flying from one commitment to the next, trying to grab enough fuel to keep hunger at bay. With that in mind, I decided to structure this book's chapters

to tackle that very crisis: Got 10 minutes before shuffling a kiddo to karate class? How about a Sunday with no commitments, but a jam-packed week looms large? Or maybe you just walked in the door and everyone needs to eat, like *now*.

Relax. I've got you covered. Here you'll find tasty solutions for every night of the week, whether you've got almost no time, a whole day to shop and cook or anything in between. You'll also find extensive suggestions and ideas for planning meals (to help alleviate the aforementioned wailing).

Sharing a meal with the people I love brings me more joy than anything else. Truly. Whether it's lightning-fast tacos or a slow-cooked lasagna, you'll never regret ending the day with a sit-down meal.

We can do this. Let's fix dinner.

A Few Words on Using These Recipes

All butter is salted. All salt is table salt. All eggs are large. Feel free to add as much or as little freshly ground black pepper or hot sauce as suits you or your brood.

15 MINUTES

NO TIME? Need to eat as soon as possible? You're in the right place. These recipes will take you from turning on the stove to that first bite of dinner in 15 minutes, and you likely have all the ingredients you need already in the fridge.

Lemony Pasta Primavera

PREP TIME 5 MINUTES | **READY IN** 15 MINUTES | **SERVES** 4 TO 5

ONE-POT PASTA TOOK the world by storm a few years ago, and with good reason. When the pasta and sauce are cooked together in one pan (yes, the pasta goes in uncooked!), the resulting dish isn't just fast and easy—it's also incredibly creamy and luxurious. As the starch cooks out of the pasta, it mixes with the water (and other yummy ingredients) to create a sauce that clings to every strand. You're going to wonder where this method has been all your life (I know I did!).

There are three important secrets to this recipe: First, you need a pasta shape that cooks in less than six minutes. Just check the package directions. Second, you need to cook this in a wide but shallow pan that can accommodate the pasta without it hanging out over the side. I use a three-inch-deep frying pan. Finally, use fat spears of asparagus. They're tastier, and they also cook in the right amount of time. Really thin asparagus will get too mushy. If you can't find any, just omit the asparagus and double the peas instead.

450-g package spaghettini

5 cups water

2 garlic cloves, minced

2 tablespoons olive oil

¾ teaspoon salt

16 asparagus spears, peeled if very woody

1 cup frozen peas

1 lemon

Grated Parmesan

1 Place the spaghettini in a large, wide frying pan or pot. The pasta should be able to lie flat, but it doesn't have to be in a single layer. Add the water, garlic, olive oil and salt. Turn the heat to high and stir the ingredients a bit (it will be difficult at this stage, since the pasta is uncooked).

2 Chop the tips off the asparagus spears and reserve. Chop the stalks into ½-inch pieces. Once the pan is boiling, cook about 2 minutes, stirring often, then stir in the asparagus pieces. Cook about 3 minutes, or until they are bright green. Add the tips and the peas and cook another 2 to 4 minutes, or until the pasta is just tender and the sauce clings to the strands. The whole process will take about 13 minutes. Remove from heat.

3 Zest the lemon over the pasta, then juice the lemon and add 1 to 2 tablespoons of the juice. Stir well and serve immediately with Parmesan.

Teriyaki Tofu with Bok Choy

PREP TIME 7 MINUTES | **READY IN** 15 MINUTES | **SERVES** 3 TO 4

¼ cup water

3 tablespoons soy sauce

2 tablespoons
brown sugar

1 to 3 teaspoons
hot chili-garlic sauce
(optional)

1 tablespoon cornstarch

450 g firm or
medium-firm tofu

1 tablespoon canola oil

1 teaspoon toasted
sesame oil

10 baby bok choy,
separated into leaves

1 tablespoon
chopped ginger

THE GREAT misapprehension about tofu is that it's a blank canvas, soaking up anything you introduce to it. Not true! Tofu actually has a subtle but distinct taste that matches perfectly with big flavours like ginger and soy, and it's so water-saturated that it really only dilutes any other ingredients you try to add it. Where tofu truly distinguishes itself is in the world of texture. It can be anywhere from silky and soft to crumbly and chewy in less than 10 minutes. What other protein can claim that?

In this recipe the tofu is cooked quickly on the stovetop and doused with a heady sauce at the last minute. I prefer a custardy but firm tofu here, so look for medium, medium-firm or firm tofu (they're all different textures, depending on the brand).

1 Stir the water, soy sauce, brown sugar, chili-garlic sauce and cornstarch together in a measuring cup.

2 Slice the tofu into 16 squares. Dry them well with paper towels (this is a losing game, as the tofu will continue to seep, but do your best with the time you have).

3 Heat a large non-stick frying pan over medium high. Add the canola and sesame oils, then add the tofu pieces. Cook about 2 minutes per side, or until they are lightly golden. Transfer the tofu slices to a serving platter.

4 Add the bok choy and ginger to the pan and cook about 2 minutes, or until bright green and tender-crisp. Stir the sauce, then add it all at once and cook, stirring constantly, until thickened, about 30 seconds. Pour the sauce and vegetables over the tofu. Serve immediately in lettuce cups or with steamed rice.

TIP You can use any quick-cooking green vegetable in place of the bok choy. I suggest shredded napa cabbage, snow peas or chopped Swiss chard.

Spiced Couscous Pilaf with Chicken

PREP TIME 10 MINUTES | **READY IN** 15 MINUTES | **SERVES** 4

ROTISSERIE CHICKEN is a boon to the time-crunched dinner maker, but it can end up being the default to just eat it plain in a salad or sandwich. This is a quick way to gussy it up—it's even nice enough to serve for a casual weeknight dinner guest. Couscous itself is another game-changer for busy evenings; it barely needs to cook, unlike pasta, rice or potatoes. Just mix it with boiling water and five minutes later you've got a filling side dish or base for a meal.

Keep this recipe in mind for summer evenings when it's just too hot to cook. Stir a cup of frozen peas into the couscous along with the currants for a hit of vegetables, if you like.

1 Heat a medium pot over medium. Add the almonds and toast gently for 2 to 3 minutes, or until fragrant. Transfer to a small bowl.

2 Add the butter to the pot, swirl it around, and then add the onion. Cook, stirring often, until softened, about 3 minutes. Stir in the cumin, cinnamon and paprika. Add the water and salt, and bring to a boil. Add the currants, then add the couscous. Stir, turn off the heat, cover and let stand 5 minutes.

3 Fluff the couscous with a fork and spread it out on a serving platter. Carve the chicken and arrange over the couscous, drizzling the chicken and couscous with any juices from the chicken container. Sprinkle with cilantro.

⅓ cup sliced almonds

2 tablespoons butter

1 small onion, finely chopped

1 teaspoon ground cumin

¼ teaspoon cinnamon

¼ teaspoon smoked paprika

1½ cups water

½ teaspoon salt

¼ cup currants or chopped apricots

1 cup couscous

1 rotisserie chicken, carved into large pieces

Chopped cilantro

Ten-Minute Tacos

PREP TIME 5 MINUTES | **READY IN** 10 MINUTES | **SERVES** 3 TO 4

1 tablespoon
ground cumin

2 teaspoons mild
chili powder

2 teaspoons cornstarch

2 teaspoons paprika

½ teaspoon
smoked paprika

½ teaspoon
garlic powder

½ teaspoon
onion powder

½ teaspoon salt

¼ teaspoon cayenne
(optional)

1 tablespoon canola oil

500 g lean ground beef

½ cup water

Taco shells, warmed

WE EAT TACOS once a week. It's a satisfying meal that we all love and that I can have on the table in less than 15 minutes. On principle, I cannot buy pre-made taco seasoning mix, but one time I accidentally bought a taco kit instead of a box of taco shells, so I used the packet of seasonings. Just my luck, my son declared those tacos the "best ever," and so began my quest to match (and improve!) packaged taco mix.

I was determined to stick within my eight essential spices (see page 168) and keep the salt to a minimum. The mix was just okay until I cracked the secret: cornstarch. Just a few teaspoons helps all the spices really cling to the meat, making the whole dish more flavourful.

We switch between hard shells and soft tortillas, and I always have lettuce cups on hand too. Our go-to toppings are pretty straightforward—sour cream, jarred salsa, sliced avocado, cilantro, grated cheddar—but top your taco however you like it best.

1 Combine the cumin, chili powder, cornstarch, paprikas, garlic and onion powders, salt and cayenne together in a small bowl. Reserve.

2 Heat a large, non-stick frying pan over medium high. Add the canola oil, then add the beef and smush it into an even layer. Cook about 3 minutes, or until the beef is more than halfway cooked (no need to stir it yet).

3 Add the spice mixture and continue to cook, now stirring and breaking up the meat, another 2 to 3 minutes, or until the beef is cooked. Stir in the water and cook another 30 seconds to 1 minute, or until the sauce thickens. Serve immediately with taco shells and toppings.

Indian Scrambled Eggs

PREP TIME 5 MINUTES | **READY IN** 12 MINUTES | **SERVES** 3 TO 4

THIS RECIPE IS so much more than just scrambled eggs. Adding the fresh onion, ginger and tomatoes, plus lots of big spices, turns a pan of eggs into a proper dinner (at least it does for me). And while I love the concept of breakfast for dinner, this just doesn't fit into the category: It's too punchy, too bold, too fabulous. I think of breakfast as a calm meal, and this is a plateful of fun. But the leftovers are outstanding warmed and wrapped in a pita bread for breakfast!

Am I overselling it? Maybe. But it's because the combination was such a revelation to me when I first tasted it. I can assure you, though, that it's worth a try at the very least. You never know, it might find a place in your weekly rotation. (Cilantro-haters, you're probably out of luck, as it's critical here. Lovers, rejoice!) If you've got a jar of hot lime pickle on hand, it makes a terrific complement here.

8 eggs

2 tablespoons butter

2 green onions, finely chopped

1 teaspoon grated fresh ginger

1 tomato, chopped

¼ teaspoon cumin

¼ teaspoon cayenne

¼ teaspoon salt

½ to 1 cup chopped fresh cilantro

Toasted pita or naan bread

1 Whisk the eggs lightly in a medium bowl. Reserve.

2 Melt the butter in a medium non-stick pan over medium high. Add the onions and ginger and cook about 1 minute. Add the tomato, cumin, cayenne and salt and cook another minute or two, or until the pan looks a bit dry. Add the eggs all at once. Use a heat-proof spatula to stir the eggs constantly, about 4 minutes, or until they are as creamy or as dry as you like them.

3 Remove from heat and stir in the cilantro. Serve with toasted pitas or naan if you like.

Sticky Korean Beef

PREP TIME 5 MINUTES | READY IN 15 MINUTES | SERVES 3 TO 4

1 tablespoon sesame oil

1 tablespoon canola oil

500 g medium or lean ground beef

2 cloves garlic, minced

1 tablespoon minced ginger

½ teaspoon hot chili flakes (optional)

2 tablespoons brown sugar

¼ cup soy sauce

4 cups thinly sliced napa cabbage

2 green onions, chopped

THIS CLASSIC KOREAN flavour combination is out-of-this-world delicious. It's traditionally made with really thinly sliced beef, but since that's time consuming and a difficult technical skill to master, I simplified it by using ground meat instead. The key here is to use a pan that is not non-stick and to let the beef cook without touching it at first so the meat gets a little bit crispy. Then, the sugar in the sauce makes the beef sticky while the other flavours meld into a dish that's basically impossible not to like.

If you have time to cook a pot of rice, it's the ideal accompaniment. If not, spoon the beef into lettuce cups or even warmed tortillas. Or just eat it with a spoon—it's that good.

1 Heat a large cast iron pan over high. Add the sesame and canola oils. Allow the oils to get really hot, then add the beef and press it into an even layer. Let it cook, without stirring, about 5 minutes, or until the edges become dark brown and slightly crispy.

2 Add the garlic, ginger and chili flakes and then stir, breaking up the larger pieces of meat, and cook another 2 to 4 minutes, or until it's mostly cooked through. If there is excess fat in the pan (this happens if you use medium ground beef), spoon out and discard some fat, leaving roughly 3 tablespoons of it in the pan.

3 Sprinkle the brown sugar over the meat and add the soy sauce. Stir well and cook about 30 seconds, then add the cabbage. Stir and cook until cabbage softens just a bit, about 3 minutes. Garnish with green onions.

Pasta with Butter and Parmesan

PREP TIME 5 MINUTES OR LESS | READY IN 15 MINUTES | SERVES 2

I'VE OFTEN SAID that the recipe for garlic spaghetti inspired my first book. For most of my life, it was the simplest dish I could imagine (it's just butter, garlic, chilies and pasta) and the epitome of my uncomplicated cooking philosophy: fast, easy, satisfying, affordable and incredibly delicious. But my son Thomas changed everything. He doesn't like the garlicky, chili-spiked pasta that my partner Michael and I so love. Instead, I make him pasta with just butter and Parmesan.

I never thought of it as a recipe—it's too simple for that—until I saw *pasta al burro* on the menu of one of the finest Italian restaurants in Toronto. Through research and testing, I stumbled upon this method, in which the cheese and butter are mashed together, thinned out with a spoonful of hot cooking water and then tossed vigorously with the pasta until the two meld into something I can only describe as magic.

It's the most delicious bowl of pasta I can imagine. It's also consistently the most popular recipe on my website. We have it about once a week, on those nights when we're cramming dinner in between school, hockey, piano and bedtime. And I'm definitely not opposed to a bowl as a late-night snack.

250 g spaghetti (about half a box)

¼ cup freshly grated Parmesan

2 tablespoons butter, at room temperature

1 Boil a large pot of water. Salt it generously. Cook the pasta according to package directions.

2 Meanwhile, mash the Parmesan and butter together in a wide serving bowl. About 1 minute before the pasta is done, ladle 2 to 3 tablespoons of the hot cooking water into the serving bowl and whisk it vigorously to combine. Use tongs to transfer the pasta directly out of the cooking water and into the serving bowl. Toss to combine well (about 30 seconds, but use your judgment) and until the sauce looks like it has been absorbed by the pasta. Serve immediately with fresh black pepper and more Parmesan.

TIP Generously salting the pasta water is critical here; without it, the whole dish is flat. I use about 1 tablespoon of salt for 4 L of water. It's worth mentioning (because this surprises many of my students) that a single portion of this pasta contains about 14 g of protein, so don't shy away from this recipe out of worry that it's not hearty enough.

Quick Lemon Chicken

PREP TIME 5 MINUTES | **READY IN** 15 MINUTES | **SERVES** 3 TO 4

2 tablespoons canola oil

750 g chicken fillets (about 12)

¼ teaspoon salt

½ cup chicken broth

Zest and juice of 1 lemon

1 tablespoon cornstarch

225 g sugar snap peas

THERE'S ONLY ONE thing to slice in this entire recipe: a lemon. Otherwise it's just heat, measure and cook, and you've got a saucy one-pot meal that's rich and lemony and tastes like it took far longer than 15 minutes. Chicken fillets are so perfect for quick meals: They cook in less than five minutes and require no chopping (so no extensive time at the cutting board). It's like you get 10 minutes back before you even start.

The secret to building flavour in the dish is to make sure the chicken develops a lovely golden colour on both sides. You achieve this by lightly drying the chicken before sautéing it, placing the fillets into oil that is already hot and letting them cook undisturbed for several minutes. Chicken fillets are sometimes called tenders, and they are the thin underside of the breast; if you can't find them, use boneless, skinless breasts cut into thick strips. Serve chicken with couscous or rice.

1 Heat a large non-stick frying pan over high. Add the oil, and then add the chicken in a single layer. Sprinkle evenly with salt and cook 2 to 3 minutes per side, or until lightly golden and cooked through.

2 While the chicken cooks, stir the chicken broth, lemon zest and juice and cornstarch together in a small bowl.

3 Add the peas to the chicken and cook until very bright green and just tender-crisp, 1 to 2 minutes. Then stir the broth mixture and add it to the pan. Cook, stirring constantly, until the sauce thickens, about 1 minute.

Sesame Ramen Salad with Chicken and Celery

PREP TIME 10 MINUTES | **READY IN** 15 MINUTES | **SERVES** 4

I HAVE TO warn you: These sesame noodles are addictive. I discovered them on a trip to New York City, where they are a mainstay on every Chinese restaurant menu. The sauce is creamy and rich but also quite spicy, which makes for a delicious contrast to the cool noodles. But to me, it's the distinctive chewiness of the ramen noodles that's behind my inability to stop at just one bowl.

These noodles are also another fun way to make a store-bought rotisserie chicken exciting and new. Don't be put off by what looks like a long list of ingredients—I'm pretty sure you already have all of these on hand, and they just need to be whisked together.

1 Cook the ramen (discard the seasoning packets) in a large pot of very well salted boiling water until just tender. Drain and rinse very well with cold tap water.

2 Combine the soy sauce, sesame oil, rice vinegar, tahini, peanut butter, honey, ginger and hot sauce in a large bowl. Whisk vigorously until emulsified. Add the noodles and toss well to coat. Add the chicken and celery and toss again.

TIP Peeling celery is one of my favourite party tricks, since it often makes people gasp with surprise and delight. It's not necessary, but it makes the stalks easier to eat. Simply run a vegetable peeler down the exterior of each stalk to remove the stringy bits that get stuck in your teeth.

3 packages
instant ramen

3 tablespoons soy sauce

2 tablespoons
toasted sesame oil

2 tablespoons
rice vinegar

2 tablespoons tahini

2 tablespoons natural
peanut butter

1 tablespoon honey

1 tablespoon
grated ginger

1 to 4 teaspoons sriracha
(optional)

2 to 3 cups shredded
rotisserie chicken

4 stalks celery, peeled
and thinly sliced

Steak and Arugula Salad with Pesto Vinaigrette

PREP TIME 5 MINUTES | **READY IN** 15 MINUTES | **SERVES** 2 TO 3

1 strip loin steak, 1½ to 2 inches thick (about 400 to 500 g)

Extra-virgin olive oil

¼ teaspoon salt

¼ cup extra-virgin olive oil

2 tablespoons fresh lemon juice

1 tablespoon pesto

½ teaspoon Dijon

¼ teaspoon salt

4 cups baby arugula

1 small chunk of Parmesan (about 2 square inches)

STEAK WITH SALAD is one of my favourite meals. It's hearty without being heavy, and I love the contrasting textures. For this recipe, I wanted to mimic a classic beef carpaccio salad—a chilled appetizer of raw beef tenderloin with arugula and Parmesan—but make it warmer and a little more substantial. The pesto dressing is delicious, not just here but on any of your other green salads.

1   Pat the steak dry with paper towels. Brush both sides lightly with olive oil, then sprinkle evenly with salt.

2   Heat a heavy frying pan over high. Place the steak in the dry pan and cook 2 minutes. Flip the steak and cook another 2 minutes, then reduce the heat to medium and cook another 5 to 8 minutes, or until the steak is medium rare to medium. Transfer to a cutting board and let rest at least 5 minutes.

3   Meanwhile, combine the oil, lemon juice, pesto, Dijon and salt in a small jar and shake well, until combined. Divide the arugula between 2 or 3 plates. Use a vegetable peeler to shave thin slices of cheese over the arugula.

4   Slice the steak thinly and divide over the salads. Drizzle with the vinaigrette.

Thai Red Curry Chicken

PREP TIME 3 MINUTES | **READY IN** 13 MINUTES | **SERVES** 3 TO 4

THIS IS THE most popular dish at most Thai restaurants (my family certainly orders it every time). Who knew you could make it at home in minutes?

Thai red curry paste comes pre-made in a little jar and just needs some coconut milk and fresh lime to round it out into a delicious, restaurant-quality sauce. In an ideal world, I'd serve this with rice to soak up the sauce, but when time is truly pinched, I serve the curry on its own in deep bowls.

1 Heat the oil in a large non-stick frying pan over high. Add the chicken in a single layer and cook about 2 minutes per side, or until the chicken is lightly golden.

2 Add the mushrooms and cook another 2 minutes, or until the mushrooms soften just a bit. Add the coconut milk and curry paste, stir well, reduce the heat to medium and bring to a simmer.

3 While the mixture is coming to a simmer, trim off the base of each bok choy and rinse the leaves well (they can trap lots of grit). Stir the individual leaves into the curry mixture. Once it boils, turn off the heat. Zest the lime overtop, then juice it and add 1 to 2 tablespoons to the mixture. Garnish with a few drops of fish sauce and some cilantro.

TIP This recipe needs just a small amount of coconut milk. Look for the little cans next to the regular-sized ones, or just use half of a regular can and freeze the rest (it freezes beautifully!).

1 tablespoon canola oil

675 g chicken fillets, cut in half

250 g sliced mushrooms

161-mL can coconut milk

3 tablespoons Thai red curry paste

6 baby bok choy

1 lime

Fish sauce

Fresh cilantro

Pasta with Tuna and Antipasto

PREP TIME 5 MINUTES | READY IN 15 MINUTES | SERVES 2 TO 3

250 g short pasta,
such as gemelli

3 80-g cans olive-oil-
packed tuna, drained

8 oil-packed sun-dried
tomatoes, thinly sliced
(about ½ cup)

⅓ cup chopped
fresh parsley

3 tablespoons
extra-virgin olive oil

Zest of 1 lemon

3 tablespoons
fresh lemon juice

Grated Parmesan

¼ cup kalamata olives

I'M DEVOTED TO oil-packed tuna. It's far superior in taste and texture to water-packed tuna—so much so that you can effortlessly build a delicious dinner around it (if you can manage not to eat it all right out of the can, but maybe that's just me). I love combining it with a few ingredients you'd find in an antipasto bar, so that every bite has a hit of intense flavour. The lemon and parsley brighten the dish, and although this is truly a meal you can throw together with almost no notice, it's elegant enough to serve at a dinner party.

If you make this with ingredients out of the pantry, there's no need to heat them up, but if they're fridge cold, simply combine the sauce ingredients in a metal bowl and perch the bowl over the boiling pasta pot for a few minutes to warm them up.

1 Cook the pasta in a large pot of boiling, well salted water until just tender, about 7 minutes, or according to the package directions.

2 While the pasta cooks, combine the tuna, sun-dried tomatoes, parsley, olive oil, lemon zest and juice in a large serving bowl. Set the bowl over the boiling pasta for 1 to 2 minutes to warm the ingredients gently.

3 As soon as the pasta is cooked, drain it and add it to the bowl. Stir very well to combine. Serve topped with freshly grated Parmesan and a few olives.

So, What's the Plan?

LET'S GO BACK to that random Wednesday afternoon, and that text message that makes you either cheerful or despondent: *What's for dinner?*

Why is that question so tough to answer, day after day?

As far as I can tell, the average person (me included) faces five stumbling blocks:

1 No ideas for what to make
2 No groceries to make whatever idea we *do* come up with
3 Short on skills or equipment
4 No time
5 Out of sync (not everyone eats the same things or at the same time)

There's a fix to all of these, but it isn't particularly glamorous or thrilling (despite the endless ideas Pinterest serves up), and some of you might audibly groan at the next two words: meal planning.

Meal planning and shopping are the two most underrated, underdiscussed and yet critical elements of getting dinner on the table.

(I wish there were as many cute Facebook videos about them as there are about recipes!)

Meal planning creates a framework to fall back on. It's the first line of defence against all the dark arts conspiring to make you order take-out, or convincing you to eat cereal standing over the kitchen sink. It puts you in the driver's seat and makes you proactive instead of reactive.

Having a plan in place knocks out stumbling blocks one and two. A good plan also takes into consideration the skills and equipment of the cook and quietly encourages the cook's progress. It also accounts for those frazzled evenings when you need dinner on the table in minutes. In the case of stumbling block number five, you'll also need a family meeting and some all-party buy-in, but it still ends up with a meal plan. (For more on dealing with an out-of-sync family, see page 140.)

I've researched and tested every meal solution around, and I keep coming back to some form of meal planning as the ultimate way to bring joy back to the daily dinner ritual. But before you throw this book across the room,

let me share the revelation that liberated me: There is no single best way to meal plan.

You could use the camp system, in which every day of the week falls into a theme (like "pasta night"). Or maybe you have time on the weekend to stock the fridge and freezer with big-batch recipes, then dish them out over the week. If your day-to-day schedule changes on a dime, you might prefer to pencil in just three or four dinners, and lean on quick pantry meals on other nights. Or maybe you prefer to fly by the seat of your dinner chair and simply rely on a well-stocked fridge and pantry to get you through.

Let's figure out how to get meal planning right for you.

The first step is joining the *Dinner, Uncomplicated* community, where you'll find all kinds of helpful ideas, fun resources and support for getting a tasty home-cooked meal on the table. Come on over to facebook.com/groups/dinneruncomplicated.

45 MINUTES OR LESS

A FEW NIGHTS a week, I can carve out 30 to 40 minutes for getting dinner ready. I call it "enjoy cooking night" and I really do, by pouring myself a little drink, turning on some great music and taking pleasure in the chopping and stirring, smelling and tasting. These recipes will never have you chained to the stove; you'll also have time to do a few other things in the kitchen, like make a vegetable side dish, load the dishwasher or enjoy a glass of wine.

Sesame Chicken Stir-Fry with Water Chestnuts

PREP TIME 15 MINUTES | **READY IN** 30 MINUTES | **SERVES** 3 TO 4

STIR-FRIES ARE, in theory, a cornerstone of weeknight cooking. What could be better than a one-pan, quick-cooking, flavour-packed dinner? In practice, however, stir-fries can rattle even an accomplished home cook. For a great stir-fry, the cooking is quick but the prep takes time. It's essential to have all the chopping and measuring done before you even turn on the stove. Once you get cooking, it all happens too fast to fit in any more prep, never mind searching the back of the pantry for a missing ingredient.

But if you can accept that one stir-fry downfall, it's a worthy addition to a meal plan. Because once the prep is done, you're good to go. And I love that if I have 15 minutes before school pick-up to get everything ready and stash it in the fridge, dinner can be on the table 15 minutes after I walk back into the kitchen.

This combination of ingredients is a particular favourite of my crunch-loving crew, with crisp celery and water chestnuts in every bite. I use my largest non-stick frying pan, which I find more effective than a wok. It's delicious in lettuce wraps or over steamed rice, but if you are serving it with rice, start the rice before the stir-fry prep.

500 g boneless, skinless chicken breasts, cubed

1 tablespoon sesame oil

¼ teaspoon salt

½ cup chicken broth

¼ cup dry white wine (or extra chicken broth)

3 tablespoons hoisin sauce

2 tablespoons cornstarch

1 to 3 teaspoons sriracha

1 tablespoon canola oil

1 red pepper, cubed

2 stalks celery, thinly sliced

2 teaspoons finely minced or grated fresh ginger

2 cloves garlic, minced

½ cup sliced water chestnuts

1 Combine the chicken, sesame oil and salt in a medium bowl. Reserve.

2 Stir the chicken broth, wine, hoisin, cornstarch and sriracha together in a measuring cup. Reserve.

3 Heat a large non-stick frying pan over high. Add the canola oil, then add the chicken. Cook, without stirring, until the chicken is golden at the edges, about 3 minutes. Stir, then add the red pepper and celery. Cook, stirring often, another 2 to 4 minutes, or until the chicken is almost totally cooked. Add the ginger and garlic and cook until the chicken is done.

4 Stir the sauce, then add it to the pan. Cook, stirring constantly, until the sauce is thickened. Stir in the water chestnuts.

Caramelized Onion Pasta with Sausage

PREP TIME 10 MINUTES | **READY IN** 35 MINUTES | **SERVES** 4 TO 5

500 g orecchiette or any short pasta

2 tablespoons canola oil

2 to 3 medium yellow onions, thinly sliced

¼ teaspoon salt

3 to 4 Italian sausages

¼ cup white wine or dry white vermouth

Grated Parmesan

THERE'S AN OLD chef's adage that claims, "Brown food tastes good." It's so true. Anything that's cooked to a caramelized, deep golden brown colour can make your mouth water before even taking a bite. Here, it's slow-cooked onions that have a starring role, with their intense sweet-bitter flavours. Sausage plays a part, but more as a supporting actor whose occasional lines set up the star for even more glory. And the brown bits from the bottom of the pan, mixed with some wine or vermouth, are the all-important soundtrack that brings the whole dish together. Warning: This dish won't photograph well, but your tummy will want its autograph.

1 Boil the pasta in a large pot of boiling salted water until tender. Drain, reserving about 1 cup of the pasta cooking water.

2 While the water boils, heat the oil in a large frying pan over medium high. Add the onions and salt, and stir well to combine. Remove the sausage meat from the casings (just squeeze it out) and add to the pan. Cook 15 minutes, stirring the onions and breaking up the sausage meat frequently, reducing the heat as necessary so the onions do not burn.

3 Once the onions are deeply golden brown, add the wine and about ¼ cup of the pasta cooking water. Cook, stirring well to scrape up and incorporate all the brown bits from the bottom of the pan, for 2 to 3 minutes. Stir in the cooked pasta, adding a bit more pasta cooking water if the sauce is too thick to coat the noodles. Serve topped with Parmesan.

Pad Thai Shrimp with Noodles

PREP TIME 10 MINUTES | **READY IN** 20 MINUTES | **SERVES** 4

THIS RECIPE IS LOOSELY based on pad Thai, but I wanted it to be lighter on the noodles and heavier on the vegetables. In the traditional dish, tamarind paste would play the role of sweet and sour, but since it can be hard to find, I substituted molasses, brown sugar and lots of fresh lime juice.

I use tiny cold-water shrimp here—they are my preference for all things shrimp since they are wild caught in North America. They are sold shelled and cooked so they only need a few minutes in the pan to get hot.

1   Boil a kettle of water. Place the noodles in a large metal or glass bowl and cover with the boiling water. Let stand about 7 minutes, or until softened and barely tender. Drain and reserve.

2   Whisk the lime zest and juice with the fish sauce, brown sugar, molasses and chili-garlic sauce. Reserve.

3   Heat a large non-stick frying pan over high. Add the oil, then add the snap peas and green onions and cook, stirring often, until the peas are bright green, 1 to 2 minutes. Stir in the shrimp and noodles. Cook 1 or 2 minutes, or until piping hot. Remove from heat and add the sauce mixture. Toss very well to combine. Divide among 4 bowls and top with peanuts.

TIP   It's easier to stir and serve the noodles if you break them in half before soaking them.

250 g wide rice noodles

Zest of 1 lime

¼ cup fresh lime juice

3 tablespoons fish sauce

2 teaspoons brown sugar

2 teaspoons molasses

2 to 4 teaspoons hot chili-garlic sauce

1 tablespoon canola oil

450 g sugar snap peas

4 green onions, thickly sliced

340 g cold-water shrimp, thawed

¼ cup roasted, salted peanuts

Cheesy Dutch Baby

PREP TIME 10 MINUTES | **READY IN** 25 MINUTES | **SERVES** 2 TO 3

4 eggs

⅔ cup all-purpose flour

⅔ cup milk

¼ teaspoon salt

⅔ cup grated old
cheddar, divided

3 tablespoons butter

2 tablespoons
extra-virgin olive oil

1 tablespoon
balsamic vinegar

⅛ teaspoon salt

4 cups mixed greens

½ cup cherry
tomatoes, cut in half

1 green onion, minced

IMAGINE A CREPE and an omelette had a love child and covered it with a tangy salad. Intrigued? Dutch baby is like a giant puffy pancake—part popover, part soufflé and all delicious. Making it feels a bit like a magic trick since you put a pan of liquid batter into the oven and in no time it blooms up into a crispy, golden puffball (kids will happily sit in front of the oven glass and watch its progress with awe).

Dutch baby is also like a distant but beloved cousin of the cheddar soufflé in my first book. It's easier and faster than soufflé, though, and while it's not as luxurious, it's still incredibly tasty and satisfying. And since it always looks like a salad bowl to me, I add greens and make it true!

1 Preheat the oven to 450°F. Whisk the eggs and flour together in a large bowl. Whisk in the milk and salt. Whisk in about half of the cheese.

2 Melt the butter in a 10-inch, oven-safe frying pan (such as cast iron—the pan cannot be non-stick) over medium. Swirl so it coats the entire bottom of the pan. Pour the egg mixture into the melted butter. Sprinkle with the remaining cheese. Transfer the pan to the oven and bake 12 to 15 minutes, or until the mixture puffs up and browns across the top.

3 While the Dutch baby cooks, whisk the oil, vinegar and salt in a large bowl until combined. Add the greens, tomatoes and onions and toss to coat. Pile the salad into the centre of the hot Dutch baby and serve immediately, cut into wedges.

Saucy Sesame Tofu with Mushrooms

PREP TIME 10 MINUTES | **READY IN** 25 MINUTES | **SERVES** 3 TO 4

I LOVE TOFU and I'm always on the hunt for new ways to enjoy it. This method of crumbling and frying it gives it the look of ground meat, and since I adore saucy ground meat stir-fries, it made sense to try the same method for tofu.

Tofu's only trouble is that every brand has a slightly different moisture content and consistency. One brand's medium could be drier than another brand's extra-firm, and that makes my job difficult: What should I call for in this recipe? The ideal tofu here is dry enough so it crumbles with some effort. Too soft and it will smush and lose its structure; too firm and you'll need a grater or knife to break it down. Instead, you want a tofu that crumbles into little irregular bits that look as though it has been ground.

Serve this in lettuce wraps or over steamed rice.

½ cup water

3 tablespoons soy sauce or tamari

2 tablespoons cornstarch

2 teaspoons granulated sugar

1 to 3 teaspoons sriracha (optional)

350-g package firm tofu

1 tablespoon canola oil

1 tablespoon toasted sesame oil

250 g white mushrooms, thinly sliced

2 stalks celery, sliced

2 green onions, minced

2 cloves garlic, minced

1 Combine water, soy sauce, cornstarch, sugar and sriracha in a small bowl or measuring cup and stir until the sugar dissolves. Using your hands, crumble the tofu into small pieces into a bowl.

2 Heat a large non-stick frying pan over medium high. Add the canola and sesame oils. Add the mushrooms and cook 3 to 5 minutes, or until they start to turn golden. Add the crumbled tofu and cook 5 to 8 minutes, or until the tofu gets browned in places.

3 Add the celery, onions and garlic and cook another 1 to 2 minutes, then stir the sauce and add it all at once. Cook, stirring constantly, until thickened, about 30 seconds. Serve immediately.

Thai Steak Salad

PREP TIME 10 MINUTES | **READY IN** 30 MINUTES | **SERVES** 4

675 g flank steak

¼ teaspoon salt

¼ teaspoon
garlic powder

¼ cup fresh lime juice

3 tablespoons canola oil

2 tablespoons
brown sugar

2 tablespoons fish sauce

1 tablespoon hot chili-
garlic sauce (optional)

142 g baby spinach
(about 8 cups, packed)

2 cups shredded
napa cabbage

1 large mango, peeled
and chopped (optional)

THAI DISHES ARE known for being pretty intense—although they are always meant to be a balance between hot, sour, salty and sweet. To me, the combination is a perfect match for a tangle of crunchy vegetables topped with sliced grilled steak. The big flavours of fish sauce, lime juice and chili sauce, mellowed by the sweetness of brown sugar, make this easy salad the dinner equivalent of a night at the disco: bright, fun and a little spicy! The mango is optional (since I know lots of people don't like fruit with their meat), but I love the tart sweetness it brings to the party.

---

1 Preheat the barbecue to high. Sprinkle the steak with the salt and garlic powder. Grease the grill, then add the steak and cook 3 to 5 minutes per side for medium rare. Transfer to a cutting board to rest for at least 5 minutes, and as much at 20 minutes.

2 Whisk the lime juice, canola oil, brown sugar, fish sauce and chili-garlic sauce together in a large bowl. Add the spinach, cabbage and mango and toss well.

3 Slice the steak thinly against the grain. Divide the salad among 4 plates and top with steak. Drizzle the steak with the dressing remaining in the bowl.

TIP Slicing flank steak against its grain is a necessary step to make each slice tender as you bite it. Look for the lines of the fibres of the meat, then slice perpendicular to those lines.

Golden Baked Wings with Creamy Dip

PREP TIME 10 MINUTES | READY IN 35 MINUTES | SERVES 3 TO 4

WHEN I WAS writing this book, Michael mentioned casually, "I hope you've put your wings in this time." The truth is, I hadn't. He blinked (maybe he squawked?), and then made the case that wings are an excellent supper—and that these wings in particular are magically easy and delicious. Soon enough I was convinced (and I'm and pretty sure one of us then popped out to procure a pack of wings for that very evening).

I prefer naked wings, with a rich, cool, creamy dip, as opposed to sauced-up Buffalo-style. Sometimes I want blue cheese dip, other times I want ranch; the recipe here can be either.

4 teaspoons baking powder

½ teaspoon salt

1 kg chicken wings, split in two

½ cup mayonnaise

⅓ cup plain yogurt

2 teaspoons fresh lemon juice

2 teaspoons Dijon

1 very small clove garlic, grated

¼ cup snipped chives or dill, or both

⅓ cup crumbled blue cheese (optional)

1 to 3 teaspoons hot sauce (optional)

1   Preheat the oven to 400°F. Line a large rimmed baking pan with foil and spray the foil with cooking spray.

2   Combine the baking powder and salt in a large bowl. Add the wings and toss very well so each wing is coated. Place on the prepared pan, skin-side-up. Roast 25 to 35 minutes, or until golden and crispy.

3   To make the dip, stir the mayonnaise, yogurt, lemon juice, Dijon, garlic and chives or dill together in a medium bowl. Stir in the blue cheese, mashing it into the sauce a bit with a fork, and then the hot sauce. The dip keeps well for up to 24 hours in the fridge.

Roasted Vegetable and Hummus Pizzas

PREP TIME 5 MINUTES | **READY IN** 20 MINUTES | **SERVES** 4

1 small head of broccoli, cut into bite-sized florets

1 red pepper, sliced

4 mushrooms, sliced

3 tablespoons extra-virgin olive oil, divided

⅛ teaspoon salt

1 cup hummus

4 7-inch pita breads

1 cup crumbled feta

2 green onions, minced

Cilantro or mint

WITHOUT APOLOGY, this is a brazen mash-up of the world's greatest topped flatbreads. It's as if pizza and tostadas and *manakeesh* all hopped into a Tilt-a-Whirl. It's fast, pretty and packed with veggies and flavour. It also gives hummus a happy new purpose—frankly, it was getting tired of just being a dip. It's pizza without being too cheesy, tostada without all the work and *manakeesh* with more veg. Feel free to use whatever roasted vegetables you like best.

1 Preheat the oven to 425°F. Line a baking sheet with parchment paper. Put the broccoli, peppers and mushrooms on the baking sheet and drizzle with 1 tablespoon of the oil. Toss well, spread into an even layer and sprinkle with the salt. Roast for 7 to 9 minutes, or until tender-crisp and sizzling. Set aside.

2 Meanwhile, spread the hummus evenly on the pita breads, then top with feta and green onions. Place the pitas on a new baking sheet (or transfer them to the first one once the vegetables are done). Divide vegetables across the tops of the pitas.

3 Bake 2 to 3 minutes, or until everything is piping hot. Take them out of the oven, drizzle with the remaining olive oil and sprinkle with cilantro or mint.

Scallion-Ginger Salmon Noodles

PREP TIME 15 MINUTES | **READY IN** 30 MINUTES | **SERVES** 4

THIS SIMPLE SCALLION sauce is a game-changer. It's zesty and delicious and easily improves fish, chicken, tofu or just plain noodles. I discovered it served in tiny plastic condiment tubs with takeout Chinese barbecue, but I quickly realized that every in-the-know chef on earth was already slathering scallion-ginger sauce on everything from oysters to scrambled eggs. It's no wonder: With this sauce, you can transform even humble packaged ramen into a glorious dinner. Feel free to substitute any leftover cooked meat, fish or tofu for the salmon.

By the way, where I live scallions are called green onions, but I like the sound of "scallion" in this recipe. I hope you'll allow it.

1   Heat the canola oil in a small pan over high. Once it's very hot, add the ginger, garlic and scallions. Cook until fragrant, about 1 minute, then transfer to a bowl. Stir in the soy sauce, vinegar and sesame oil. Reserve.

2   Preheat the broiler to high and make sure 1 rack is about 7 inches below the element. Line a small rimmed baking pan with foil. Place the salmon on the baking sheet and sprinkle with salt. Broil 5 minutes, or until the salmon is golden on the top edges. Remove from the oven and let rest 5 minutes.

3   Cook the ramen in boiling salted water for 2 minutes. Stir in the edamame and cook another minute, or until the ramen is just tender. Divide the noodles among 4 bowls and toss each portion with about a tablespoon of the sauce. Flake the salmon into large pieces and divide among the bowls. Drizzle the salmon with the remaining sauce.

¼ cup canola oil

3 tablespoons chopped fresh ginger

3 cloves garlic, minced

¾ cup sliced scallions (about 1 bunch)

2 tablespoons soy sauce

1 teaspoon rice or white wine vinegar

½ teaspoon toasted sesame oil

450 g skinless salmon fillets

⅛ teaspoon salt

4 packages ramen (discard seasoning packets)

1 cup shelled edamame

Juicy Herbed Turkey Burgers

PREP TIME 10 MINUTES | **READY IN** 20 MINUTES | **SERVES** 4

1 onion

½ cup panko

3 tablespoons Dijon

1 tablespoon Worcestershire sauce

¼ teaspoon dried thyme (optional)

¼ teaspoon salt

450 g ground turkey

Canola oil

I TOOK A deep dive into turkey burgers one hot summer day. I'd never had one that was really juicy and yummy, so I was determined to puzzle out a perfect recipe. The internet is full of zany suggestions, and I tried many of them, including adding mayo to the burger mix (this was not a win). In the end, I leaned on my tried-and-true burger tricks—adding grated onion for flavour and moisture, and including Dijon for punch.

I also made peace with the fact that turkey burgers need soft, unassuming buns. This isn't the time for a crusty, multi-seed rye roll, which just overwhelms the burger's delicate flavour. Ketchup, mustard, lettuce and tomato are welcome, as always.

MAKE IT AHEAD Shape the burgers and freeze them, separated by squares of parchment, for up to 2 months. Thaw overnight in the fridge.

1 Grate the onion, using the large holes of a box grater, into a large bowl. Add the panko, Dijon, Worcestershire, thyme and salt and stir well. Add the turkey and mix very well to combine.

2 Shape the mixture into 4 equal patties, making them very flat and about ½ an inch wider than the buns.

3 Preheat the barbecue to medium high. Spray or brush it generously with canola oil. Add the burgers and cook 3 to 5 minutes per side, or until cooked through and springy to the touch. Serve on buns with the usual condiments.

TIP If you can find all dark meat ground turkey, snap it up! It makes the tastiest and best-textured burgers.

Our Favourite Pork Chops

PREP TIME 5 MINUTES | **READY IN** 20 MINUTES | **SERVES** 3 TO 4

OUR SON THOMAS is a meat lover. Many of his dinners are 90% meat (with a bit of toast and some raw vegetables to make his mother happy). For a while, on nights when I wasn't home for supper, he and Michael would have boys' night pork chops, and the next morning at breakfast I always heard about how good they were. So one evening I asked Michael to make them while I watched (and took notes!). In his typical, wonderful way, they could hardly have been simpler... or more delicious. They're not just a boys' night meal anymore—they're a weekly staple.

Serve these with Perfect Mashed Potatoes (page 176) and Crunchy Coleslaw (page 173), or take a cue from Thomas and just add toast and raw veg.

4 boneless pork loin chops, each about 1½ inches thick

1 tablespoon canola oil, divided

¼ teaspoon salt, divided

¼ cup dry white vermouth

Chopped fresh parsley (optional)

Freshly ground black pepper

1 Preheat the oven to 400°F. Heat a cast iron frying pan over high. Brush the pork chops on one side with about half of the canola oil and sprinkle with about half the salt. Add to the pan once it's very hot, oil-side-down. Brush the tops with the remaining oil and sprinkle with the remaining salt. Cook 2 minutes, then flip and transfer the pork chops to a small baking sheet. Bake 3 to 5 minutes, or until just cooked (about 150°F internal temperature or until its juices are faintly pink).

2 Meanwhile, reduce the heat under the frying pan to medium. Add the vermouth and stir, scraping up the browned bits to create a pan sauce and simmering until it thickens slightly. Once the chops are cooked, add them back into the frying pan, turning to coat in the sauce. Sprinkle with parsley and pepper.

Sweet and Sour
Eggplant Caponata

PREP TIME 15 MINUTES | **READY IN** 50 MINUTES | **SERVES** 4 TO 6

4 tablespoons canola oil

1 medium red
onion, sliced

¾ teaspoon salt

1 large eggplant
(about 825 g)

2 red peppers, sliced

3 cloves garlic, sliced

¼ teaspoon chili
flakes (optional)

156-mL can
tomato paste

1 cup water

⅓ cup chopped fresh
parsley (optional)

⅓ cup chopped,
pitted kalamata olives

2 tablespoons
extra-virgin olive oil

1 tablespoon
balsamic vinegar

1 tablespoon capers

EGGPLANT AREN'T BITTER—though they have every right to be, with all the mean things people say about them. Still, they remain a hard sell to many, and I completely understand. It was a running joke in my family that, although my favourite colour was purple, I couldn't stand eggplant. For years I received eggplant-themed joke gifts: tea towels, notecards and even a beautiful whistling kettle shaped like an eggplant (its lid was the green stem!). Despite this, I still wouldn't eat it. It seemed spongy but not tender, and unpleasantly bland.

But then, in my early 20s, I met two different eggplant dishes that changed everything. The first, Sheet Pan Eggplant Parmesan, is on page 81. The second is this southern Italian classic. It's creamy, hearty and comforting but somehow also elegant. In Italy, this is served as a side dish or condiment, but I love it as a main, served over pasta, polenta or toast.

Needless to say, I have become a fervent eggplant lover. If only I hadn't sold that gorgeous kettle so many years ago.

1 Heat the canola oil in a large, wide pot over medium. Add the onions and salt. Stir well and cook, covered, until they are just starting to soften, about 5 minutes.

2 Trim off the top of the eggplant. Cut it in quarters lengthwise, then cut each quarter into ½-inch slices. Add the eggplant to the onions and cook, covered, until it starts to soften and break down, about 5 minutes. Stir in the peppers, garlic and chili flakes, reduce heat to low and cook, covered, until the peppers start to soften and the mixture starts to look a bit wet, about 5 minutes. Stir in the tomato paste and water, then cover and simmer very gently for 15 to 20 minutes, or until the eggplant is completely soft (poke a slice, it should yield easily).

3 Remove from heat and stir in the parsley, olives, olive oil, vinegar and capers. Serve immediately or at room temperature.

Make Meal Planning Work for You

I'D BE WILLING to bet that you know your Myers-Briggs type or your Enneagram number (at some point, the internet serves up those quizzes for us all). But do you know what type of meal planner you are?

That's right, there's more than one way to plan your meals (including not really planning them at all). This was a light-bulb moment for me. The best way to map your meals for the week depends on your personality, your day-to-day schedule and responsibilities, your family structure and so much more. My best way isn't yours, and vice versa, and the secret to making meal planning work is to do it however is best *for you*.

Personally, I bristle at rules. I'm the person silently thinking, "You can't tell me what to do" after a barista calls, "Have a great day!" so programming every meal makes me feel trapped and angry. Before I woke up to this reality, I tried again and again to plot out my week and stick to the plan. But by Tuesday or Wednesday, I'd rip up the list and spend an hour trying to decide what to make for dinner instead. It wasn't the best use of my time (what with all the planning, ripping up and re-planning!).

So, I spoke to lots of home cooks about this and gleaned their methods. Everyone gave me different ideas, and what became clear is that there are different ways to meal plan, all with the aim of alleviating the dinnertime scramble. From my observations, there are five types of meal planner:

1 **The Classic:** Wakes up Sunday morning, consults Paprika, Pinterest or cookbooks, writes up the week of meals and an air-tight shopping list. Shops, then sticks to the plan. *Great for:* Organized people with predictable schedules. *Not great for:* Anyone who has a problem with authority (hi!).

2 **The Camper:** Assigns a theme or protein to every night of the week, just like at summer camp! Taco Tuesdays, Chicken Wednesdays, Vegan Thursdays, and so on. The recipes can change from week to week but the themes or proteins repeat. *Great for:* People who like a bit of structure but don't want to plan every meal in detail. *Not great for:* Anyone who really dislikes repetition.

3 **The Batcher:** Spends a day making a few key dishes in large quantities, then freezes them in meal-sized portions. Pulls a frozen pouch out of the freezer every morning. *Great for:* People who love to spend one entire day a week in the kitchen. People with chest freezers. People with long commutes or who have very little prep time for dinner. People who often eat out of sync with the rest of the household. *Not great for:* People with tiny freezers. People who easily tire of the same meal.

4 The Semi: Pencils in three or four meals for the week. Cooks those meals at some point during the week, maybe, and leans on back-pocket dinners the other nights of the week. *Great for:* People whose schedules change on a dime. People who write cookbooks but still need to feed their family and not lose their minds. *Not great for:* People who have no time to think until the weekend.

5 The Wingnut: Cooks according to mood. There's no plan, but the pantry is full of options. Constantly bookmarking recipes online and in cookbooks to try someday. *Great for:* Young couples. Retired chefs. *Not great for:* Most of the rest of us.

Which type are you? Which one would you like to be? (You can even be a combination of types.)

I'm mostly a Semi, but with a bit of Camper and Batcher. I write a few meal ideas on an erasable whiteboard on our fridge, making sure to slot in my son's favourites (Ten-Minute Tacos, page 18, and Upside-Down Chicken with Preserved Lemon, page 86). Most weeks I'm working on recipes, and sometimes those can be our dinner (unless I'm testing three types of cheesecake!). Michael is English, so he's happiest when Sundays are "Roast Dinner Night," which could be anything from a chicken to a pot roast, as long as it's served with some kind of potatoes. On a day when I know we'll be rushing, I often reach into the freezer for a batch of something like Brothy Beans (page 128).

As long as I take five to 10 minutes at the beginning of the week to loosely map out a few things (emphasis on loosely to satisfy my inner rebel), I am less anxious and flustered during the week, and that's what meal planning is all about!

Maybe you love themes and you're more of a Camper. Perhaps the Classic is the best fit for

your busy but organized life. Even if you're a Wingnut—or perhaps an Accidental Wingnut, as I was for many, many years—there are still lots of ways to reduce the scramble of the daily dinner-time routine.

Take a few minutes to think about what meal-planning type makes sense for your life, and then turn to page 92 for my tips, tricks and tweaks.

I'd also like to extend a special invitation to join our *Dinner, Uncomplicated* community, where you'll find all kinds of helpful ideas and fun resources, as well as a supportive group of Classics, Campers, Batchers, Semis and Wing-nuts all doing their best to get a tasty meal on the table most nights of the week. Come join us at facebook.com/groups/dinneruncomplicated.

SET IT AND FORGET IT

THESE RECIPES deliver an enormous return on a small investment. With less than 15 minutes of prep time, followed by either a spell in the slow cooker or up to an hour in the oven, the meals in this chapter will give you layers of flavour with barely any work.

Roasted Vegetables with Chickpeas

PREP TIME 10 MINUTES | **READY IN** ABOUT 1 HOUR | **SERVES** 4

THERE'S A FABULOUS potato-and-vegetable side dish recipe in an old Italian cookbook of my mom's. We often had it with our Sunday roast dinners, but it always struck me as being nearly hearty enough to serve as a main course. A can of chickpeas and some optional cheese fill in the gaps and make this a rich casserole of sorts (which also happens to be gluten-free and potentially vegan!).

Cut all the vegetables into similarly sized wedges. By the time the potatoes and onions are tender, the peppers and tomatoes will be roasted to caramelized yumminess.

1 Preheat the oven to 425°F. Combine the peppers, potatoes, tomatoes, onion, chickpeas, olive oil and salt in a 9 × 13-inch casserole dish. Roast 30 minutes, then stir everything well; reduce the oven to 400°F and roast another 20 to 30 minutes, or until the potatoes are tender and the other vegetables are golden at the edges.

2 Sprinkle with cheese and roast 3 to 5 minutes, or until the cheese softens. Drizzle with another little bit of olive oil and sprinkle with parsley just before serving.

2 red peppers,
cut into wedges

2 medium red-skinned
potatoes, cut into
thin wedges

2 large tomatoes,
cut into wedges

1 large yellow or white
onion, cut into wedges

540-mL can chickpeas,
drained and rinsed

¼ cup extra-virgin
olive oil

1 teaspoon salt

½ cup crumbled feta or
goat cheese (optional)

Chopped fresh parsley

Roasted Sausage and Vegetable Gnocchi

PREP TIME 15 MINUTES | **READY IN** 75 MINUTES | **SERVES** 4

2 Italian sausages

1 small onion, chopped

1 red pepper, chopped

250 g mushrooms, chopped

796-mL can whole plum tomatoes

500-g package potato gnocchi

¼ teaspoon salt

⅓ cup 35% cream

1½ cups shredded mozzarella

MEET YOUR NEW favourite comfort food. This is similar to a classic baked pasta casserole but 10 times easier and faster. It's so satisfying, warming and ooey-gooey that it would be worth hours of stovetop fussing, but instead, it's all made in the oven with almost no work.

Roasting the meat and vegetables together in a baking dish makes the base for an intensely flavourful sauce. Then just stir in store-bought gnocchi, cover and bake, and you've got a modern twist on lasagna. It's the perfect dinner for a chilly, dark night (and it will also make you the most beloved guest at any potluck!).

1 Preheat the oven to 400°F. Spray a medium baking dish with cooking spray. Squeeze the sausage meat out of the casing and place in the prepared dish (discard the casing). Add the onion, pepper and mushrooms. Stir very well. Roast for 20 to 25 minutes, or until the meat is brown and bubbly.

2 While the sausage and vegetables roast, drain the tomatoes into a large bowl (save the liquid separately). Crush the tomatoes (either with your hands or with a potato masher). Stir in the gnocchi and salt. Reserve.

3 Take the dish out of the oven and reduce the temperature to 350°F. Use a wooden spoon to break up the meat, then stir everything together again. Stir in the gnocchi mixture and mix well. Spread into an even layer. (The gnocchi should be partially covered with liquid; if not, add some of the reserved tomato liquid.) Cover tightly with foil and bake 20 minutes, then remove the foil, stir and bake another 20 minutes uncovered or until the entire mixture is bubbly.

4 Stir in the cream. Sprinkle with mozzarella cheese and bake, uncovered, another 5 to 10 minutes, or until the cheese melts and starts to brown. Let stand at least 5 minutes before serving.

TIP Look for packaged gnocchi in the pasta aisle or in the deli.

Provençal Fish Soup

PREP TIME 15 MINUTES | **READY IN** 45 MINUTES | **SERVES** 4 TO 5

I'D LOVE TO EAT more fish but getting it fresh is challenging, so I'm always looking for ways to use the frozen white fish fillets that are easy to pick up at any grocery store. They can be fiddly to cook, but this is the easiest and most foolproof way to do it, since it's so gentle that the fish doesn't overcook at all. Simply drop the fillets into a delicious soup and simmer them very gently until they're cooked enough to break into flakes. No chopping, no stress!

This is a French-inspired soup so I use *herbes de Provence*—a blend of green herbs and lavender—but you can substitute a half teaspoon each of dried thyme and rosemary.

1 Heat the oil in a large pot over medium high. Add the leeks, fennel and salt and cook, stirring often, about 5 minutes, or until the vegetables are translucent. Stir in the diced potato, *herbes de Provence* and chili flakes. Add the broth, passata and wine. Bring to a boil then reduce heat to low, cover and simmer very gently for 25 minutes or until the potatoes are tender.

2 Add the fish fillets, making sure they are fully submerged. Cover the pot and return to a gentle simmer. Cook 5 to 10 minutes, or until the fish flakes easily with a spoon.

2 tablespoons canola oil

1 leek, sliced into
thin half moons

1 fennel bulb, chopped

½ teaspoon salt

1 medium Yukon Gold
potato, peeled and diced

1 teaspoon *herbes
de Provence*

⅛ teaspoon chili flakes
(optional)

3 cups fish or
chicken broth

680-mL jar tomato
passata (about 2½ cups)

½ cup dry white wine

400 g frozen skinless
white fish fillets (such
as haddock)

Slow Cooker Butter Tofu

PREP TIME 15 MINUTES | READY IN 4 HOURS | SERVES 6

1 cup plain yogurt

2 tablespoons
lemon juice

1 tablespoon turmeric

1 teaspoon grated
fresh ginger

2 400-g packages
firm or extra-firm tofu

⅓ cup butter

1 medium onion, minced

2 cloves garlic, minced

2 teaspoons
ground cumin

1¼ teaspoons salt

⅛ teaspoon cayenne
(optional)

⅛ teaspoon cinnamon

680-mL jar tomato
passata (about 2½ cups)

¼ cup 35% cream

½ teaspoon
garam masala

Fresh cilantro

WHY DOES CHICKEN get to have all the fun? Famous and velvety butter chicken sauce works just as well with tofu, and gently simmering it in the slow cooker is the ideal way to infuse the tofu with as much of its deliciousness as possible. The tofu slowly releases liquid, which gets replaced by the rich sauce. It's important not to use non-fat or low-fat yogurt here because it will split when it cooks. Look for at least 4% plain, traditional yogurt (don't use Greek yogurt!). Feel free to add 1½ cups of frozen peas along with the cream. Cover and cook until hot.

1 Stir the yogurt, lemon juice, turmeric and ginger together in the slow cooker. Cut the tofu into 1-inch cubes and add to the yogurt mixture. Stir very gently.

2 Melt the butter in a large non-stick frying pan over medium. Add the onion and cook about 2 minutes, or until fragrant. Add the garlic, cumin, salt, cayenne and cinnamon and cook another 2 minutes. Stir in the passata. Pour this mixture over the tofu in the slow cooker and stir very gently. Cover and cook on high for 4 hours.

3 Gently stir in the cream. Serve over rice, sprinkled with a little garam masala and fresh cilantro.

TIP No slow cooker? Marinate the tofu as above for 20 minutes. Cook the onion and spice mixture in a medium pot. After adding the passata, bring to a boil, then reduce heat to simmer. Gently stir in the tofu and its marinade. Cover and simmer very gently for 15 minutes. Stir in the cream.

Buttery Brown Sugar Salmon

PREP TIME 10 MINUTES | **READY IN** 45 MINUTES | **SERVES** 4

THIS RECIPE WAS inspired by a photo I saw somewhere online of beautifully roasted salmon slathered with grainy mustard—it looked so delicious that it stuck with me. Through trial and error, I realized that just using the mustard isn't enough to make salmon delicious; it also needs some sweetness and fat. And since there is always brown sugar and butter in my kitchen—and it's a winning combination in other recipes—I gave it a whirl. It still wasn't quite as exciting as I had imagined, so I tried my old "soak it in white wine" trick. Presto. A beautiful, sweet-and-savoury broiled salmon. Serve with crispy Brussels Sprouts with Bacon (page 172).

½ cup dry white wine

4 salmon fillets (about 600 g total)

3 tablespoons brown sugar

3 tablespoons butter, melted

3 tablespoons grainy mustard

⅛ teaspoon salt

1 Place the wine in a small baking dish. Add the salmon skin-side-up. Marinate at room temperature for 30 minutes.

2 Stir the brown sugar together with the butter, mustard and salt in a small bowl until combined. Reserve.

3 Preheat the oven to 400°F. Line a large rimmed baking pan with foil and lightly spray the foil. Place the salmon skin-side-down on the prepared pan (discard the marinade). Sprinkle with salt. Smear the brown sugar mixture over the top of each fillet. Roast 12 to 15 minutes, or until it feels springy and flakes easily with a fork.

Crispy Chicken with Leeks and Fennel

PREP TIME 10 MINUTES | READY IN 40 MINUTES | SERVES 3 TO 4

1 large leek, trimmed

1 fennel bulb, trimmed

2 tablespoons canola oil, divided

½ teaspoon salt, divided

6 bone-in, skin-on chicken thighs

½ cup whole green olives

¼ cup chopped fresh dill

I DEVELOPED AN appreciation for chicken thighs only recently. While many food fiends are adamantly pro-dark meat, I was an outlier who preferred the breast. As with all things to do with chicken, it was Michael who changed my mind. He loves to take a hot lunch to work and often roasts an entire pan of chicken thighs to portion out for a week. He just puts a family pack of bone-in thighs on a pan, salts them like crazy and roasts them at a high heat. These no-fuss, no-muss thighs are juicy, with irresistibly crispy skin. Thomas and I both fell in love, and they are now part of our regular dinner rotation.

Being me, I always feel compelled to add vegetables to the pan. Fennel and leeks are so often overlooked, but they are perfect here. They cook and caramelize in just the right amount of time and subtly complement the simple, delicious chicken. A handful of green olives adds an unexpected burst of tanginess.

1 Preheat the oven to 425°F. Line a large rimmed baking sheet with parchment or foil. Slice the leek in half lengthwise and cut into ¼-inch half moons. Trim, halve and core the fennel, and slice crosswise into ¼-inch half moons. Combine on the prepared baking sheet. Add 1 tablespoon of the oil and toss well. Spread in an even layer in the middle of the baking sheet. Sprinkle with ¼ teaspoon of the salt.

2 Place the chicken skin-side-up around the edge of the pan. Brush with the remaining oil and sprinkle with the remaining salt. Roast 30 to 35 minutes, or until the chicken is golden and the vegetables are very tender.

3 Sprinkle with green olives and cook another minute or two. Sprinkle with dill.

Sheet Pan Eggplant Parmesan

PREP TIME 10 MINUTES | **READY IN** ABOUT 1 HOUR | **SERVES** 3 TO 4

CONFESSION: I'VE NEVER made authentic eggplant Parmesan. Anything that needs to be salted, rinsed, dried, battered and fried in small batches loses me at the second step. But I adore all of its flavours, and since eggplant roasts into creamy deliciousness as long as it has the time it needs in the oven, a sheet pan preparation seemed perfectly suited to the concept. This works beautifully as a vegetarian main course, served with bread and a big salad.

I tend to use good quality, store-bought marinara sauce if I don't have any of my own homemade sauce on hand. Look for ones with as few ingredients as possible. For this recipe, you'll want eggplant that are roughly the same width from top to bottom. The ones that are very bottom-heavy tend to be more seedy. I love the skin, but you can peel the eggplant if you don't. Finally, don't be tempted to skimp on the oil—it's the key to making the eggplant luxuriously tender.

2 large eggplant

½ cup canola oil, divided

¾ tsp salt

1¼ cups marinara sauce

340-g ball mozzarella, thinly sliced

¼ cup grated Parmesan

Fresh basil leaves

1 Preheat the oven to 400°F. Line two large rimmed baking pans with parchment paper. Slice the eggplant into 1-inch rounds and divide between the two sheets (you should have about 15 slices). Using about ⅓ cup of the canola oil, brush both sides of each slice and sprinkle with salt.

2 Roast for 30 minutes, each pan on its own oven rack, then flip the eggplant and drizzle with the remaining 2 tablespoons of oil. Switch the pans on the racks, then roast another 10 to 15 minutes, or until the eggplant is golden on both sides.

3 Transfer all the eggplant slices to one pan, snuggling them right up next to each other. Preheat the broiler to high. Spoon marinara sauce overtop the eggplant, then top with sliced mozzarella. Sprinkle with Parmesan. Broil 2 to 5 minutes, or until the cheese is melted and golden. Garnish with fresh basil before serving.

Slow Cooker Chicken Taco Chili

PREP TIME 10 MINUTES | **READY IN** 5 HOURS | **SERVES** 4 TO 6

796-mL can whole tomatoes

1 tablespoon brown sugar

2 teaspoons smoked paprika

1 teaspoon onion powder

1 teaspoon garlic powder

1 teaspoon salt

¼ teaspoon chili flakes (optional)

6 boneless, skinless chicken thighs (about 650 g)

540-mL can black beans, drained and rinsed

2 cups frozen corn

3 tablespoons fresh lime juice

THIS RECIPE WAS a happy accident. I was slow-cooking chicken thighs for tacos one day but I added way too much liquid, so I got a thick soup instead of saucy pulled chicken. So, I added some corn and a can of black beans and we had a hearty chili with all of our favorite Tex-Mex flavours, and instead of serving it in tacos, I served it with tortilla chips. You can also offer sour cream, hot sauce and cilantro for topping.

Chicken thighs are richer than breasts so they're much better for slow-cooking. Breasts become unpleasantly dry.

1 Combine the tomatoes, brown sugar, paprika, onion and garlic powders, salt and chili flakes in a slow cooker. Crush with a potato masher or purée with an immersion blender. Add the chicken, turning it over to get every surface coated with the sauce.

2 Cover and cook on high for 4 hours (it can switch to warm and rest for several hours after cooking if that suits your timing).

3 Use two forks to loosely shred the chicken. Stir in the beans, corn and lime juice, and cook until piping hot.

Skillet Turkey Meatloaf

PREP TIME 10 MINUTES | **READY IN** 50 MINUTES | **SERVES** 6 TO 8

MEATLOAF IS HAVING a renaissance. It's on all kinds of restaurant menus, it was easily one of the most popular recipes in my first book and it generally seems to have shuffled off its reputation as a dreary dish from another era. This is great news for home cooks who have been quietly cooking meatloaf to general applause for years: Now we can shout about it!

Turkey meatloaf needs a bit of help in the flavour and moisture departments, since the meat sold these days is so lean. I've added fresh mushrooms and onion—but don't worry, they don't need to be chopped or pre-cooked, you can just grate them into a bowl and be on your way. To speed things up a titch, I bake meatloaf in my big cast iron frying pan. This might negate its status as a loaf, but it's equally delicious (maybe even more so, since each slice has a generous coat of ketchup) and cuts the cooking time in half. Feel free to bake this in a 9 × 5-inch loaf pan for about 70 minutes instead, if the folks at your table demand true meatloaf. Serve with baked potatoes, buttered egg noodles or toast and a simple vegetable like Hot Honeyed Sweet Potatoes (page 177).

1 cup panko breadcrumbs

¾ cup milk or cream

2 eggs

1 tablespoon Worcestershire sauce

1 teaspoon salt

½ teaspoon dried thyme

½ teaspoon granulated garlic

6 cremini mushrooms

1 medium onion

900 g ground turkey

2 tablespoons canola oil

½ cup ketchup or barbecue sauce

1 Preheat the oven to 400°F. Combine the panko and milk in a medium bowl and let stand for 5 minutes. Whisk in the eggs, Worcestershire sauce, salt, thyme and garlic. Then grate the mushrooms and the onion, using the large holes of a standard box grater, and add them to the bowl. Add the turkey and stir until the mixture is completely combined.

2 Brush a 10-inch, oven-safe skillet with the canola oil, then add the turkey mixture and gently pack it into an even layer (make sure it touches the sides too). Brush the top with ketchup or barbecue sauce.

3 Bake 10 minutes, then reduce the heat to 350°F and cook another 20 to 35 minutes, or until the blade of a paring knife poked into the centre of the loaf is hot to the touch. Let stand 5 minutes before cutting into wedges to serve.

Upside-Down Chicken with Preserved Lemon

PREP TIME 5 MINUTES | **READY IN** 1 HOUR | **SERVES** 3 TO 4

6 bone-in, skin-on chicken thighs

¼ teaspoon salt

1 tablespoon canola oil

1 lemon

½ teaspoon salt

½ teaspoon sugar

THIS IS A chef's trick for cooking duck breasts, but I'm borrowing it for chicken thighs. By cooking the chicken skin-side-down over low heat for a long time, the fat just underneath the skin melts slowly while the skin becomes golden and crispy. But not only that, this dish also takes less than 10 minutes to prepare, then happily bubbles away quietly without needing any tending to whatsoever. Oh, baby!

It doesn't need anything else to make it a solid-gold superstar recipe, but I snuck in a tiny bit of quick-preserved lemon for a surprise burst of tanginess. Serve this with Creamy Polenta (page 173) and Golden Cauliflower with Tahini Sauce (page 175).

1 Pat the chicken very dry with paper towels then sprinkle salt all over the skin. Heat a large cast iron frying pan over low (it should accommodate all the chicken without the pieces touching each other). Add the oil and swirl the pan to coat the bottom. Place the chicken skin-side-down in the pan. Cook, without disturbing the chicken too much, for 35 to 45 minutes, or until the skin is deeply golden. Regulate the heat so the chicken bubbles and is crackling quietly but constantly. Carefully turn over the chicken pieces and cook another 5 to 10 minutes, or until cooked through. Transfer to a serving platter.

2 While the chicken cooks, use a vegetable peeler to take 5 long strips of lemon zest off the lemon. Then squeeze the lemon and combine the zest and juice in a small bowl. Stir in the salt and sugar and let stand while the chicken cooks.

3 After transferring the chicken to a serving platter, take the lemon zest out of the juice mixture and chop it finely. Add the chopped zest plus 1 to 2 tablespoons of the juice mixture to the frying pan. Stir well, scraping up the brown bits from the bottom of the pan. Drizzle the sauce over the chicken.

TIP If possible, leave the chicken uncovered in the fridge overnight before cooking—it helps dry out the skin so it can get more crispy.

Slow Cooker Chili

PREP TIME 22 MINUTES | **READY IN** 8 HOURS | **SERVES** 8 TO 10

THERE SEEM TO be many life occasions that call for a big batch of great chili: potlucks, game nights, Sunday dinners, skating parties, victory parties, divorce parties. You get the idea. And it's even better when it can be made in advance and kept warm and waiting in the slow cooker. Chili is comfort food appropriate for casual gatherings, or you can dress it up with lots of pretty toppings for a dinner party. I've made many a pot of chili for all of these occasions, and this is my all-time favourite recipe. It's spiced without being too spicy, and it seems to have just the right amount of vegetables to make everyone happy (including my selective seven-year-old!). Don't be put off by what looks like a long list of ingredients—I bet you have almost everything in the pantry already.

I serve this with rice, baked potatoes or bread. Having a buffet of toppings makes it feel really special too. Some of my favourites are sour cream, sliced avocado, fresh cilantro, grated cheddar, hot sauce and tortilla chips.

---

1 Heat large, wide frying pan over medium high. Add the canola oil. Add the beef and press it into an even layer. Cook the beef, without stirring, about 5 minutes, or until the underside is golden brown. Break up the beef into small pieces, then scrape it into a slow cooker insert, leaving one or two tablespoons of fat behind in the frying pan.

2 Return the pan to the heat and add the onions, carrots, garlic and salt. Cook, stirring often, until the vegetables start to soften, about 4 minutes. Stir in the cumin, chili powder, smoked paprika, garlic powder, onion powder and cinnamon. Cook about 1 minute, then add the liquid from the tomato cans and stir. Let this mixture cook for a few minutes.

3 Crush the tomatoes (with either your hands or a potato masher) and add to the slow cooker. Add the tomato paste, peppers, kidney beans, beef broth and cocoa powder. Add the onion mixture from the pan. Stir thoroughly to combine. Cover and cook on low for 8 hours.

TIP No slow cooker? Make this on the stovetop, and double the amount of beef broth. Simmer for about 40 minutes.

2 tablespoons canola oil

1 kg lean ground beef

1 large onion, diced

3 carrots, diced

4 cloves garlic, minced

½ teaspoon salt

2 tablespoons ground cumin

2 tablespoons chili powder

1 teaspoon smoked paprika

½ teaspoon garlic powder

½ teaspoon onion powder

⅛ teaspoon cinnamon

2 796-mL cans whole tomatoes

156-mL can tomato paste

1 red pepper, chopped

1 green pepper, chopped

2 540-mL cans red kidney beans, drained and rinsed

1 cup beef broth

1 tablespoon unsweetened cocoa powder

Sheet Pan Pork Tenderloin with Onions and Bacon

PREP TIME 10 MINUTES | **READY IN** 45 MINUTES | **SERVES** 3 TO 4

12 to 16 baby potatoes, cut in half

1 large yellow onion, very thickly sliced

2 slices bacon, chopped

2 tablespoons canola oil, divided

750 g pork tenderloin

¼ teaspoon dried thyme

¼ teaspoon salt, divided

I WENT THROUGH a long phase of making dinner by combining ingredients on a sheet pan and tossing the whole thing in the oven for 40 minutes. There were successes and failures. But the day I added chopped bacon to the mix really caused a sensation in my house. It doesn't take much bacon to skyrocket a ho-hum sheet pan supper into the stratosphere of solid-gold suppers. This combination here of bacon, onions and potatoes is so delicious and smells so intoxicating that I could almost skip the tenderloin. But then again, it's such a favourite, and such an easy, quick and stress-free cut to cook, that it's the perfect centrepiece for this (and many other!) sheet pan wonders.

1 Preheat the oven to 425°F. Line a large rimmed baking pan with parchment or foil. (If using foil, spray the foil with cooking spray.) Put the potatoes, onions and bacon on the prepared pan, along with 1 tablespoon of the oil, and toss very well to combine. Spread the mixture out in an even layer across the whole pan, leaving lots of space in the middle for the pork.

2 Dry the pork with paper towels, then put it in the middle of the baking sheet. Brush the pork with 1 tablespoon of the oil and sprinkle it with the thyme and about half of the salt. Sprinkle the rest of the salt over the potato mixture.

3 Roast for 25 to 30 minutes, stirring the onions and potatoes halfway, or until onions and potatoes are tender and pork is cooked. Let the pork rest for 5 to 10 minutes before slicing and serving.

Things Smart Cooks Do

NOT ONLY HAVE I been making dinner for myself for almost 30 years, I've also been teaching cooking for more than 20! From hacking my own methods to watching my students come up with ingenious ideas, I've compiled 10 simple ways to make cooking dinner easier, faster and more delicious.

1 Make a plan. Take 20 minutes once a week (or double that if you only want to do it once a month) and write out your meal plan or theme nights (you'll want to work out which type of meal planner you are first, so read page 64).

2 Know your family's favourite meals. Keep a list, and update it. I don't know why this simple thing makes the first barrier about 10 times easier to overcome, but it really does (I keep ours on a piece of paper on the fridge).

3 Know three really fast meals by heart and always keep the pantry stocked with their ingredients. These are your fail-safes, so you can still whip up dinner even though a long commute or a sick child made your original plan fall through. Mine are Pasta with Butter and Parmesan (page 25), Ten-Minute Tacos (page 18) and Cheesy Dutch Baby (page 46).

4 Equip your kitchen for easy, fun cooking. My full list of essentials is on page 168, but the two items that make everyday cooking immeasurably better are a decent cutting board and a good knife. Personally, I prefer wood or bamboo for the former and an 8-inch chef's knife for the latter.

5 Anchor your cutting board with a few wet paper towels. Tucked underneath, they keep that board from rocking, wiggling, moving around or being otherwise frustrating. It's amazing how much faster (and safer) chopping is when the cutting board is secure. A thin, wet dish cloth or piece of grippy, non-stick shelf liner both work well too.

6 Keep your knife sharp—remember that sharp knives actually prevent cuts—by using a home knife sharpener and with annual trips to a professional sharpener. There are lots of inexpensive guided knife sharpeners available that are perfect for home use.

7 Keep a compost bowl handy, right next to the cutting board to collect vegetable trimmings. It saves time and energy by cutting down on trips to the bin (which, in my house, also means fewer potato peels on the floor). It also keeps your cutting surface open and tidy, which makes chopping faster, safer and more precise.

8 Use salt. Salt the pasta cooking water; salt the beans when they're soaking; salt the meat before and after cooking. Food tastes so much better when it's properly salted.

9 Eat what's in the house before cooking anything new. Save money and time by creating a meal from what's in the pantry. Repurpose leftovers. Reheat that stew that's in the freezer. For lots more tips on reducing food waste, read page 120.

10 Buy a rotisserie chicken (or whatever your preferred shortcut is). Make a salad and add the shredded chicken. Drizzle it with olive oil and balsamic vinegar and dinner is done in 10 minutes and you didn't even turn on the oven. You still made dinner, you superstar.

Remember that no one—truly, no one—is hoping for a gourmet, multi-course meal. At the end of the day, all we want is comfort. Familiar, uncomplicated food that consoles us. Forget fancy and fussy and just cook. And if dinner's a disaster, don't fret—you've got another chance tomorrow.

Don't forget to come join our community of smart cooks to share and learn many more tips and tricks. Click over to facebook.com/groups/dinneruncomplicated.

MAKE IT AHEAD

WHEN LIFE GRANTS you some extra time that isn't during the working-parent witching hours of 4 to 7 p.m., you can use it to get a jump on dinner. Here are some of my favourite recipes that either freeze or refrigerate very well without affecting the final flavour or texture.

Glazed Ginger Chicken Meatballs

PREP TIME 25 MINUTES | **READY IN** ABOUT 1 HOUR | **SERVES** 6 TO 8

THESE MEATBALLS WERE inspired by battered and deep-fried Chinese chicken balls. My son adores them (though it's possible it's just the electric-pink sauce he loves) so I wanted to try to capture the essence of their deliciousness without the batter or the deep-frying. (I also made it my mission to create a glorious glaze that isn't fluorescent.) These are all that and more: The onions, ginger and garlic make them intensely flavourful, and the milk-soaked panko—a trick I borrowed from Italian meatballs—makes them really tender and juicy. Serve these with rice and Roasted Miso Eggplant (page 177), or bring them to your next potluck.

MAKE IT AHEAD Instead of chilling the meatballs in the fridge, freeze them on the baking pan. Once fully frozen, transfer them to a storage container and keep frozen for up to 2 months. To cook, thaw in the fridge overnight and cook as above, or cook directly from frozen: Bake at 350°F for 20 minutes, then add the ketchup mixture and broil for 3 to 6 minutes, or until bubbly.

1 cup panko

½ cup milk

1 kg ground chicken

2 eggs

4 green onions, finely chopped (about ½ cup)

3 large cloves garlic, minced

1 tablespoon minced ginger

2 teaspoons sesame oil

½ teaspoon salt

½ cup ketchup

2 tablespoons honey

2 tablespoons soy sauce

¼ teaspoon ground ginger

1 tablespoon canola oil

1 Stir the panko with the milk in a large bowl. Let it soak for 2 minutes, then add the chicken, eggs, green onions, garlic, ginger, sesame oil and salt. Stir very well to combine.

2 Line a large rimmed baking pan with parchment. Wet your hands with cold water, then shape the chicken mixture into about 24 large meatballs. Place them on the prepared pan. Cover lightly with plastic wrap and chill in the fridge for at least 30 minutes, and for as long as 12 hours.

3 Stir the ketchup, honey, soy sauce and ginger together in a small bowl. Preheat the broiler to high, making sure the top rack is about 8 to 10 inches below the element. Line a large baking pan with foil and spray or brush with oil. Transfer the chilled meatballs to the greased pan. Brush each one with some canola oil. Broil 5 to 7 minutes or until golden and bubbling. Carefully turn each meatball over and broil another 2 minutes. Spoon a little of the ketchup mixture over each meatball and broil another 1 to 3 minutes, or until the glaze is bubbly.

Lemon and Garlic Chicken Kebabs

PREP TIME 15 MINUTES | **READY IN** 50 MINUTES | **SERVES** 4

1 lemon

¼ cup lemon juice

2 large garlic
cloves, peeled and
coarsely chopped

1 teaspoon
dried oregano

½ teaspoon salt

6 boneless, skinless
chicken thighs
(about 675 g)

Extra-virgin olive oil

IT'S STILL ASTONISHING to me just how much flavour you can squeeze out of one lemon. (Sorry, I couldn't resist.) This marinade looks too easy but, while ease is never a bad thing in my books, it really delivers on taste too. I like to make up these skewers and stash them in the freezer. The marinade does its work both while the chicken freezes and again when it thaws, and having the meat already skewered makes life for future me so much easier. Serve with couscous and Crunchy Coleslaw (page 173).

MAKE IT AHEAD Freeze the skewered chicken for up to 4 weeks. Thaw in the fridge overnight before cooking.

---

1 Set the skewers in cold water and leave to soak for at least 10 minutes.

2 Use a vegetable peeler to remove the lemon zest in long pieces, and drop them into a large freezer bag or container. Add the lemon juice, garlic, oregano and salt and stir to mix.

3 Cut the chicken into big cubes. Thread 5 cubes of chicken on each skewer, nestling them quite close to each other. Trim the pointed ends of the skewers so they fit into the marinating bag or container, then place the skewers in the marinade and roll them around to coat each one. Close up the bag or container and marinate at room temperature for 20 minutes, or for up to 2 hours in the fridge.

3 Preheat the grill to high. Grease the grill very well, then add the skewers. Grill with the lid closed for 2 minutes, then then flip the skewers, close the lid again and grill another 2 minutes. Reduce the heat to medium low, then close the lid and grill another 8 to 10 minutes, or until cooked through and springy to the touch. Take skewers off the grill and drizzle with olive oil.

TIP You can use three boneless, skinless chicken breasts instead of thighs if that is your preference. Just reduce the cooking time a little bit.

Chickpea and Rosemary Nut Burgers

PREP TIME 10 MINUTES | **READY IN** 20 MINUTES | **SERVES** 6

I STARTED MY professional cooking career in 1997 in a small, refined restaurant in Ottawa. At that time, plant-based eating wasn't even a twinkle in anyone's eye, and we had just one token non-meat item on the menu. It was never a big seller. As such, it often fell to me, the novice, to make. Anxious to prove myself, I did extensive research after-hours, diving deep into Ayurvedic and macrobiotic cooking, as well as old issues of *Gourmet*. One day I came up with something similar to these burgers, a blend of chickpeas, nuts and rosemary; it was listed on our menu with the unfortunate name of "Nut Burger." It wasn't a great seller, but my chef loved it. It earned me one of his rare but sincere compliments, and so it remains a treasured recipe to me.

It's important not to drain the chickpeas for this. Their liquid, called aquafaba, is a terrific binder and replaces the eggs I originally used.

MAKE IT AHEAD Shape the patties and stack two-high with a square of parchment in between. Tuck them into a freezer bag and freeze for up to 3 months. To use, thaw overnight in the fridge.

Ingredients

540-mL can chickpeas (not drained)

1 cup sliced almonds, toasted

1 cup panko

1 large garlic clove

1 green onion, chopped

1 tablespoon coarsely chopped rosemary leaves

½ teaspoon salt

Zest of 1 lemon

2 tablespoons fresh lemon juice

2 tablespoons extra-virgin olive oil

Canola oil

1 Combine all of the ingredients, except the canola oil, in a food processor. Purée until smooth. Shape into 6 patties (the mixture will be sticky, and shaping the patties is easier with slightly wet hands) and place on a parchment-lined baking dish. Chill at least 20 minutes, and for as long as 24 hours.

2 Heat a large non-stick frying pan over medium high. Brush each patty with a little canola oil and add to the pan. Cook about 2 minutes per side, or until golden, then reduce the heat to low and cook another 5 to 7 minutes, or until piping hot (poke a small knife or metal skewer into the centre of the patty and then place the utensil on your lower lip—it should feel very warm). Serve on buns with sliced tomatoes, onions and condiments.

Creamy Chicken and Vegetable Pot Pie

PREP TIME 40 MINUTES | **READY IN** 50 MINUTES | **SERVES** 6

4 cups chicken broth

750 g boneless, skinless chicken thighs or breasts

⅓ cup butter

1 medium onion, chopped

3 stalks celery, chopped

2 carrots, finely chopped

½ cup all-purpose flour

1 teaspoon dried thyme

1 teaspoon salt

Freshly ground black pepper

1½ cups frozen peas

1 teaspoon Dijon

THE BEST GIFT I received after our son was born (actually, I'd say it's in the top five gifts I've received in my life) was a chicken pot pie. My friend Jane came over to meet wee Thomas with the pie and a bag of salad mix for our dinner. It was during those bleary, sleepless newborn weeks, and that delicious pie made me feel so cozy and comforted that I'll remember it fondly forever.

The classic filling is simple but rich and creamy, and it's versatile too. There are many ways to make it into a pie of sorts. I like it simply baked with biscuits on top, like a cobbler (or with my Flaky Biscuits on page 174 alongside). Others insist it needs a pastry top and bottom. I've also had the luxurious filling ladled over fresh waffles, spooned into puff pastry cups, sandwiched between two slices of toast and served in a bowl like a stew. The point is, make this filling and do with it what you will. No matter what, it will always be comfort food at its finest.

MAKE IT AHEAD Make the filling, cool and keep chilled up to 48 hours. Reheat gently on the stove or in a slow cooker.

1 Combine the chicken broth and chicken in a medium pot. Bring to a simmer over medium heat. Once simmering, cover and continue to simmer very gently until cooked through, about 10 to 15 minutes. Remove the chicken and let cool. Transfer the broth to a large liquid measuring cup and reserve.

2 Melt the butter in a large pot over medium. Add the onion and cook, stirring occasionally, 5 minutes, or until starting to soften. Add the celery and carrots and cook another 5 to 7 minutes, or until the vegetables are tender. Sprinkle the flour over the vegetables, then stir until all the veg is coated.

3 Add about 1 cup of the reserved chicken broth. Once it incorporates and starts to thicken, stir in another cup. Repeat, reserving about 1 cup of broth. Stir in the thyme and salt, and season with pepper. Cook the pot pie mixture over medium, stirring often and scraping the bottom of the pot, until it just starts to boil gently. Stir in the peas and Dijon.

4 Shred or chop the chicken into large bite-sized pieces and fold it into the mixture.

TIP After cooking the chicken initially, there may be some solid bits of protein left in the broth. This is normal, and you can incorporate them into the sauce.

Tandoori-ish Chicken

PREP TIME 10 MINUTES | **READY IN** 6½ HOURS | **SERVES** 4

THERE ARE TWO secrets to tandoori chicken: a long marinade in spiced yogurt, and blistering heat. It's traditionally cooked in a clay oven at about 850°F, but don't worry—a standard home oven at 450°F can still produce a delicious dinner. I skip the red food colouring that's often added for effect in restaurants and replace it with double the turmeric. This is a wonderfully simple marinade, and cooking chicken breasts for a short time at a high heat makes them quite juicy.

Use high-fat yogurt (not Greek) for this recipe—it makes the chicken juicier and more flavourful, and it's less likely to scorch in the oven. I like to serve this chicken with basmati rice or naan and a salad of chopped cucumbers, tomatoes and red onions; I also add store-bought hot lime pickle or sweet mango chutney to the table.

4 small boneless, skinless chicken breasts (about 1 kg total)

1 cup plain yogurt

2 tablespoons canola oil

2 teaspoons coriander

1 teaspoon cumin

1 teaspoon smoked paprika

1 teaspoon turmeric

½ teaspoon salt

½ teaspoon ground ginger

¼ teaspoon cayenne (optional)

⅛ teaspoon cinnamon

Lime wedges and fresh mint (optional)

1 Place the chicken in a baking dish or freezer bag. Combine the yogurt, oil, coriander, cumin, smoked paprika, turmeric, salt, ginger, cayenne and cinnamon in a small bowl. Pour over the chicken and roll the chicken around so it gets completely coated. Refrigerate for at least 6 hours, and for as long as 24 hours.

2 Preheat the oven to 450°F, placing a rack in the middle of the oven. Line a large rimmed baking pan with foil and lightly spray the foil with oil. Place the chicken on the pan, trying to keep as much marinade on it as possible.

3 Roast 15 minutes, then turn the broiler to high, leaving the pan in the middle of the oven. Broil, checking the chicken often, for 3 to 6 minutes, or until the marinade looks a little golden here and there and the chicken is cooked through. Let stand 5 minutes before serving. Garnish with lime wedges and mint.

Mushroom and Lentil Ragu

PREP TIME 25 MINUTES | **READY IN** ABOUT 1 HOUR | **SERVES 6**

14 g dried porcini mushrooms

1 cup boiling water

2 tablespoons canola oil

1 medium yellow onion, finely chopped

3 stalks celery, finely chopped

1 teaspoon salt

500 g white mushrooms (about 20)

3 large cloves garlic, minced

796-mL can whole tomatoes

1 cup dry white wine

156-mL can tomato paste

540-mL can lentils, drained

1 teaspoon finely chopped fresh rosemary

¼ cup extra-virgin olive oil

***Pangritata* (optional)**

THIS VEGAN RECIPE probably seems a long way from beefy bolognese sauce, but that's what inspired it. There's no meat, butter, milk or cheese here, but with a rich sauce flavoured by wine and by fresh and dried mushrooms, this dish has a similar vibe. I treat it the same way and serve it over pasta or Creamy Polenta (page 173).

I like to leave about half of this sauce un-puréed to show off the lentils, but it can also be fully puréed if there is a lentil skeptic at your table. The crispy *pangritata* garnish (can't go wrong with breadcrumbs!) is optional but so fun, and a great way to use up stale bread.

MAKE IT AHEAD Freeze the sauce for up to 3 months. Thaw overnight in the fridge, then reheat.

1 Place the dried mushrooms in a medium bowl and pour 1 cup of boiling water over them. Stir and let stand for 10 minutes. Fish out the mushrooms and save the soaking liquid. Chop the mushrooms finely. Reserve.

2 Heat the canola oil in a large, wide pot over medium low. Add the onions, celery and salt; cook, stirring often, until the onions are nearly translucent and a bit golden, about 10 minutes. While that's cooking, grate the white mushrooms on the large holes of a box grater (if you're left with any big chunks just give them a quick chop). Add the white mushrooms and garlic to the onion mixture. Increase the heat to medium and cook, stirring often, until the mushrooms release their moisture and the mixture becomes mostly dry, about 10 minutes.

2 Add the mushroom soaking liquid to the pot, keeping back any sediment left in the bottom of the bowl. Crush the tomatoes, with scissors or your hands, and then add them and their juices to the pot along with the wine, tomato paste, lentils, rosemary and reserved chopped rehydrated mushrooms. Bring to a boil, then reduce heat and simmer vigorously, uncovered, for about 30 minutes, or until the sauce thickens.

3 Purée about half of the mixture (either purée partly with an immersion blender, or take some out, purée in a blender and add it back to the pot). Stir in the olive oil. Serve over pasta or polenta and sprinkle with *pangritata*.

TIP *Pangritata* is known as "poor man's Parmesan" in Italy, but it's an ingenious, vegan way to add a sprinkle of flavour and texture where you might usually use Parmesan. To make it, process one or two slices of stale bread in a blender until it's in coarse crumbs. For one cup of breadcrumbs, heat ¼ cup of extra-virgin olive oil in a small pan over medium high. Add the breadcrumbs and cook, stirring often, until the breadcrumbs are dark golden and crispy (anywhere from 1 to 5 minutes). Drain on paper towels and sprinkle with a bit of salt. This can be made up to 24 hours in advance. Sprinkle over the ragu just before serving.

Turkey Chili Verde

PREP TIME 20 MINUTES | **READY IN** 40 MINUTES | **SERVES** 5 TO 6

THIS IS A DIFFERENT take on classic tomato-based beef chili. It still has lots of vegetables, beans, spices and meat, but it's different enough to be a completely fresh experience. Salsa verde is made from tomatillos, and it's easy to find in the grocery store (it's usually right next to the jarred salsa and taco shells). It's slightly more delicate and acidic than red salsa, which makes it a perfect match for turkey. I like to serve it with an abundance of tortilla chips, or spooned over a baked potato, and to top it off with sour cream, avocado and cilantro.

MAKE IT AHEAD Cook the chili and cool it completely in the fridge. Divide into 4-cup portions and freeze up to 2 months. Thaw overnight in the fridge before reheating and serving.

---

1 Heat the oil in a large pot over medium high. Add the onion, celery and salt and cook, stirring often, until the vegetables become almost translucent, about 5 minutes. Add the turkey, breaking it up with a spoon. Cook, stirring often to crumble the meat, about 5 minutes, or until it has lost its pink colour.

2 Stir in the cumin and garlic powder. Add the salsa verde, water, beans and corn. Bring to a boil, then reduce heat and simmer 10 to 15 minutes, or until the chili thickens a bit. Serve with a dollop of sour cream, some sliced avocado, cilantro and tortilla chips.

2 tablespoons canola oil

1 large onion, chopped

2 stalks celery, chopped

½ teaspoon salt

675 g ground turkey

1 tablespoon cumin

½ teaspoon garlic powder

453-g jar salsa verde (about 2 cups)

2 cups water

540-mL can white kidney beans, drained and rinsed

1 cup frozen corn

Barbecued Miami Ribs

PREP TIME 10 MINUTES | **READY IN** ABOUT 2 HOURS | **SERVES** 4 TO 6

½ cup soy sauce

¼ cup brown sugar

1 tablespoon
chopped fresh ginger

1 tablespoon
sriracha (optional)

2 teaspoons
toasted sesame oil

2 large garlic cloves,
peeled and sliced

1.2 kg Miami-style
beef short ribs

I MAKE THESE TASTY, sizzling, sticky-sweet ribs for almost every summer party we have and there are never, ever leftovers. Miami ribs are beef short ribs cut across several bones. They're usually as long as a piece of bacon and about three times as thick. They're an unusual but divine combination of tender and chewy and, when marinated like this, they become the hit of any dinner.

These are best cooked over the intense heat of wood charcoal, but a gas barbecue is fine too; just make sure to let them cook undisturbed for several minutes before attempting to flip them. (Yes, this means they'll likely stick to the grill a bit, so I cook them almost-through on one side before scraping the grill and turning over.) Serve with rice or a rice noodle salad with lots of fresh herbs.

MAKE IT AHEAD Marinate the ribs up to 24 hours in the fridge, or freeze in the marinade for up to 1 month. Thaw in the fridge overnight before cooking.

1 Combine the soy sauce, brown sugar, ginger, sriracha, sesame oil and garlic in a freezer bag or container. Stir until the sugar dissolves. Add the ribs. Marinate in the fridge for at least 2 hours, and for as long as 24 hours.

2 Preheat the grill to high. Grease the grill well with cooking spray, then add the ribs. Cook 5 minutes, or until sizzling and dark brown on the edges of the underside. Use a metal spatula to scrape between the meat and the grill, then flip the meat and cook for another 2 to 3 minutes for medium rare.

Spicy Salmon Cakes

PREP TIME 15 MINUTES | **READY IN** 25 MINUTES | **SERVES** 2 TO 3

I ONCE BELIEVED canned salmon was a tough sell. I now know better, since my inbox is flooded with grateful emails every time I develop a recipe for it. These crispy little patties are my own personal favourite. They're delicious and a cinch to whip up—plus they're a great way to have fish without the stress of shopping for fresh.

I use salmon that is packed with its skin and bones (they mash into nothingness and contribute to the dish's calcium and good fats) but if that's unthinkable, feel free to use an equal amount of the boneless, skinless salmon. Hot lime pickle is an Indian chutney sold in many grocery stores. It's also delicious served alongside any number of recipes, from Indian Scrambled Eggs (page 21) to Chickpea and Rosemary Nut Burgers (page 101).

MAKE IT AHEAD Shape the patties and freeze them in a single layer on a small parchment-lined baking sheet. Once fully frozen, tuck the patties into a freezer bag and freeze for up to 3 months. To use, thaw overnight in the fridge.

1 egg

½ cup cream or milk

213-g can salmon, drained

¾ cup panko

1 small onion, very finely chopped

¼ cup finely chopped Indian hot lime pickle

¼ teaspoon salt

1 tablespoon canola oil

1 Whisk the egg and cream together in a large bowl. Add the salmon and mash it up with a fork. Add the panko, onion, lime pickle and salt and stir very well to combine. Shape into 4 small patties.

2 Heat a large non-stick frying pan over medium high. Add the canola oil, and let it heat for 30 seconds or so. Add the patties. Cook 2 minutes, then flip patties over and cook another 4 to 6 minutes, lowering the heat as required, until cooked through.

Spiced Beef Koftas with Tzatziki

PREP TIME 10 MINUTES | **READY IN** 25 MINUTES | **SERVES** 3 TO 4

500 g lean ground beef

½ teaspoon salt

¼ teaspoon coriander

¼ teaspoon cumin

⅛ teaspoon cinnamon

⅛ teaspoon ground ginger

⅛ teaspoon onion powder

1 tablespoon canola oil

Pita breads

---

1 mini cucumber

⅛ teaspoon salt

½ cup sour cream

¼ cup chopped fresh dill or mint

⅛ teaspoon garlic powder

Tabasco sauce (optional)

WHEN THOMAS WAS about four years old, we realized he would eat almost anything that was cooked on skewers. You can imagine what happened: We promptly starting barbecuing "something on a stick" multiple nights a week. Michael came up with this one—a subtly spiced beef kebab inspired by the kofta at our favourite Turkish restaurant. (Kofta is a sort of meatball, so the mixture lent itself well to the skewer demand.) We all loved it, especially served in warm pita breads with cool tzatziki. Thomas eventually got over his skewer phase, and I can't say I'm not grateful—our barbecue skewers are too long for any of our frying pans, so kebabbing everything was a difficult wish to grant in the winter. Now I make this recipe indoors, in little oval patties, which is closer to the original dish that inspired it. Feel free to add red onion, cucumber, fresh tomatoes and lettuce to the pitas.

MAKE IT AHEAD Mix and shape the koftas and freeze in a single layer on a baking sheet. Once fully frozen, transfer them to a freezer bag. Thaw overnight in the fridge before cooking.

1 Preheat the oven to 350°F. Combine the beef with the salt, coriander, cumin, cinnamon, ginger and onion powder and stir well. Shape into 6 flat oval patties.

2 Heat the oil in a large oven-safe frying pan over medium high. Add the patties and cook 1 to 2 minutes per side, or until golden. Transfer the pan to the oven and cook about 10 minutes, or until cooked through. Serve with tzatziki in warmed pita breads.

3 For the tzatziki, peel and grate 1 mini cucumber and combine it with the salt in a colander. Let stand 10 minutes, then squeeze out as much liquid as you can. Mix the cucumber with the sour cream, fresh dill or mint, garlic powder and, if you like, several drops of Tabasco in a small bowl.

Coconut and Lime Sweet Potato Dal

PREP TIME 10 MINUTES | **READY IN** 45 MINUTES | **SERVES** 4 TO 6

EATING A BOWL of this colourful soup always makes me so happy. It's deeply satisfying thanks to the richness of lentils (really, you don't need anything alongside to feel totally full), and the combination of coconut, sweet potato and tons of fresh lime juice makes it uplifting.

If you're the kind of person who loves to have a stash of hearty soups in the freezer (and really, who isn't?), bookmark this one. Make a pot, portion it into 1½-cup freezer bags and freeze them flat. You're set not just for dinner but also for grab-and-go lunches, late-night hangries and any other meal-requiring surprises that might come along.

MAKE IT AHEAD Make the dal and cool it completely in the fridge. Divide into portions and freeze flat in freezer bags. Keep frozen up to 3 months. Thaw overnight in the fridge before reheating gently and serving.

1 Combine the lentils, sweet potatoes and water in a large pot. Stir in the curry powder, ginger, salt, turmeric, cumin, chili flakes and cinnamon. Bring to a boil, stirring often and watching carefully, since lentils have a tendency to boil over in the blink of an eye. Reduce the heat, cover and simmer very gently, stirring often, until the lentils and sweet potatoes are very soft, about 35 minutes.

2 Purée the soup or, if you prefer, skip and leave it chunky. Either way, stir in the coconut milk and lime juice. Lentils are notoriously greedy about salt, so taste it to make sure there's enough. Garnish with cilantro and a lime wedge if you like.

1½ cups red lentils

2 large sweet potatoes, peeled and chopped (about 625 g)

6 cups water

1 tablespoon curry powder

2 teaspoons ground ginger

1½ teaspoons salt

1 teaspoon turmeric (optional)

1 teaspoon ground cumin

¼ to 1 teaspoon chili flakes (optional)

¼ teaspoon cinnamon

400-mL can coconut milk

2 tablespoons fresh lime juice

Fresh cilantro and lime wedges (optional)

Modern Sloppy Joes

PREP TIME 20 MINUTES | **READY IN** 45 MINUTES | **SERVES** 4

1 tablespoon canola oil

1 onion, finely chopped

2 stalks celery,
finely chopped

½ teaspoon salt

3 cloves garlic, minced

500 g lean ground beef

680-mL jar
tomato passata

540-mL can lentils,
rinsed and drained

1½ cups beef broth

156-mL can
tomato paste

2 tablespoons
brown sugar

2 tablespoons
Worcestershire sauce

4 large buns, toasted

ONE OF MY university roommates introduced me to sloppy joes. He browned a pound of beef, added a can of sauce, and then shovelled the mixture into puny hamburger buns. At that time, I had lofty ideas about food and wasn't terribly impressed. But, like retro meatloaf or tuna casserole, sloppy joes are now back on the scene—usually with a fresher approach (it helps that I've grown up and stopped being so particular too). Thank goodness! Sloppy joes are easy, inexpensive, fast and loved by almost everyone. To modernize mine, I switch out half the beef for a can of small brown lentils. The lentils soak up the sauce and deliver a mighty dose of fibre and other goodness. Feel free to go 100% beef—or 100% lentils! Either way, this delightfully messy meal is welcome on my table any time.

MAKE IT AHEAD Make the beef and lentil mixture, then cool completely and pack into a large freezer bag. Flatten the bag to remove the air. Freeze up to 2 months. To use, thaw overnight in the fridge, then simmer until piping hot.

1 Heat the oil in a large non-stick frying pan over medium. Add the onion, celery and salt and cook, stirring often, until the vegetables soften, about 5 minutes. Add the garlic and cook another minute. Add the beef, increase the heat to high and cook without stirring for 3 to 5 minutes, or until the beef becomes golden on the bottom. Stir well, breaking up the beef into little bits, then add the passata, lentils, beef broth, tomato paste and brown sugar.

2 Bring to a boil, then reduce heat and simmer, stirring often, for 10 minutes or until the mixture thickens a bit. Stir in the Worcestershire sauce. Serve on toasted buns.

Waste Naught

WASTE SOMETIMES feel inevitable in a busy home kitchen. When we're shopping and cooking and living, the occasional head of lettuce gets forgotten in the crisper, or a container of chicken stew gets lost at the back of the fridge.

But even if it's inevitable, it still frustrates me! I'm trying to get better at reducing food waste at our house. To help you do the same, here are some tricks I've learned along the way.

1   Meal planning. By this point, you won't be surprised to hear that planning is one of the best ways to cut down on food waste. When you shop with a plan, you're less likely to buy a head of kale that will ultimately never get eaten.

2   Eat vegetables according to shelf life. Delicate items like salad greens, fresh herbs, peas and peppers should be eaten within 2 to 3 days. Hardier veg like cabbage, beets, kale and carrots can last in the fridge much longer. If you're deciding between making a green salad or a coleslaw, always make the green salad first.

3   Treat best-before dates as a guideline, not a rule. These aren't "death occurs to those who eat this item after this date." More likely the item simply isn't quite as fresh, but fully safe to eat. Obviously, use your senses and your judgment to know when something is off and should be tossed.

4   Once a week, eat from the fridge and pantry. Use up what's in there.

5   Reinvent leftovers to make them more exciting. (Jump to Second Act, below, for more on that!)

Second Act

Generally, I love having leftovers around. It certainly makes lunch easier. But when it comes to dinner, we get tired of eating the same dish (especially when I've made enough to feed 30 instead of three). To combat Leftover Fatigue (it's a thing), try one of the following recipes.

Bubble and Squeak

Mince leftovers and mix with about an equal amount of mashed potatoes, some minced green onion and a few dashes of curry or chili powder. Shape into patties and pan-fry in a little oil. Top with a fried or poached egg.

GREAT TO USE UP: leftover Indian Scrambled Eggs (page 21), Roasted Vegetables with Chickpeas (page 69), Modern Sloppy Joes (page 118).

Omelette

Mix leftovers with 1 to 2 beaten eggs per person. Cook gently in a small non-stick frying pan.

GREAT TO USE UP: leftover Pasta with Butter and Parmesan (page 25), Caramelized Onion Pasta with Sausage (page 42), Lemony Braised Leeks (page 176).

Fried Rice

Sauté leftovers with chopped onion, garlic and ginger in a non-stick frying pan. Add about ¾ cup cooked rice per person and cook until hot. Make some space in the middle of the pan and add 2 to 4 beaten eggs. Stir and cook until eggs are incorporated. Drizzle with soy sauce and sesame oil.

GREAT TO USE UP: leftover Upside-Down Chicken with Preserved Lemon (page 86), Sticky Korean Beef (page 22), Buttery Brown Sugar Salmon (page 77).

Tacos

Chop leftovers and sauté with minced onion and garlic. Add a spoonful of chili powder and a splash of wine or water. Spoon into tacos.

GREAT TO USE UP: leftover Skillet Turkey Meatloaf (page 85), Thai Steak Salad (page 50),

Sheet Pan Pork Tenderloin with Onions and Bacon (page 90), Spiced Beef Koftas (page 114).

Casserole

Add an equal quantity of cooked pasta to your leftovers, sprinkle with cheese and bake in a casserole dish until piping hot.

GREAT TO USE UP: leftover Sweet and Sour Eggplant Caponata (page 62), Slow Cooker Chili (page 89), Mushroom and Lentil Ragu (page 106).

SUNDAY STASH

SOMETIMES JUST HAVING the major building blocks for a meal can be all you need to make dinner a cinch. These big-batch basics are the beginning of a dozen delicious recipes, and they're all different so you won't get bored. Carve out some time to stock the freezer and you're all set.

Parsley Pesto

PREP TIME 10 MINUTES | **READY IN** 10 MINUTES | **MAKES** 12–15 SERVINGS (3 CUPS)

1½ cups walnut halves or almonds

2 bunches flat-leaf parsley, thick stems trimmed

1½ cups canola oil

4 tablespoons fresh lemon juice

1 clove garlic, cut in quarters

1½ teaspoons salt

DESPITE MANY ATTEMPTS to grow fresh basil in my garden, I've only ever had one crop that produced enough of the herb for a big batch of pesto (and store-bought basil is never tasty enough for a proper pesto). Parsley, on the other hand, doesn't just thrive in my garden, it's basically rampant—and it's also available at the grocery store any time of year. After trying my usual pesto made with parsley instead of basil, I was hooked. It's delicious, versatile, easy and affordable.

If you've made traditional pesto before, you might be surprised that I use neither extra-virgin olive oil nor Parmesan in the base recipe. Instead, I like to add those flavourful (and pricier) ingredients only when I use the pesto, to maximize their punch.

Use this pesto with tomatoes and mozzarella to jazz up chicken breasts, tuck it into calzones along with some ham and cheese or simply add it to pasta along with an easy green vegetable and call it a day.

To use the pesto, thaw it either overnight in the fridge or for an hour at room temperature.

1 Preheat the oven to 400°F. Place the nuts in a single layer on a small baking pan. Roast for 5 to 8 minutes, or until they are just starting to become golden and fragrant. Let cool for at least 5 minutes.

2 Wash and dry the parsley in a salad spinner, then chop it very coarsely (it should measure about 7 cups, packed). Place in a large blender and add the toasted nuts, oil, lemon juice, garlic and salt. Blend on high until completely puréed.

3 Package into 3 1-cup portions in freezer bags. Squeeze out all of the air and freeze up to 3 months. Thaw overnight in the fridge before using.

Cheesy Pesto Chicken

Preheat the oven to 400°F. Line a baking sheet with foil and place **4 boneless, skinless chicken breasts** on it. Brush the chicken with **1 tablespoon canola oil** and sprinkle with **¼ teaspoon salt**. Spoon **¼ cup Parsley Pesto** over the chicken. Top with **½ cup grated mozzarella**, then place **two slices of plum tomato** on each one. Sprinkle each one with **1 tablespoon grated Parmesan**. Bake 15 minutes, then turn the broiler to high and broil 1 to 2 minutes, or until the cheese is golden. SERVES 4.

Pesto Pasta and Greens

Boil **450 g fettuccini** in a large pot of very well salted boiling water until just tender, about 11 minutes (or according to package directions). Add **142 g baby spinach** (about 8 cups), stir it once or twice to wilt it, then drain everything and return it all to the pot. Add **1 cup Parsley Pesto, ½ cup grated Parmesan** and **¼ cup extra-virgin olive oil** and toss very well to combine. Serve sprinkled with more **Parmesan**. SERVES 4 TO 5.

Pesto and Ham Calzones

Preheat the oven to 425°F. Line a baking sheet with parchment paper. Divide a **700-g ball of raw pizza dough** into 5 equal pieces. Roll one into a 6-inch circle. Spoon about **1 tablespoon Parsley Pesto** along the bottom half of the circle. Top with **1 slice ham**, **2 slices tomato** and **2 tablespoons grated mozzarella**. Fold over the top of the dough and crimp the edges together with a fork. Transfer to the prepared baking sheet, then poke a few holes in the top of the calzone. Brush the top with **extra-virgin olive oil**. Repeat with the remaining dough. Bake 15 minutes, or until dough is golden. SERVES 5.

Brothy Beans

PREP TIME 10 MINUTES | READY IN 7 HOURS | MAKES ABOUT 8 SERVINGS

750 g dried beans, such as Great Northern or Romano (about 4 cups)

2½ teaspoons salt, divided

1 large onion, sliced

3 stalks celery, coarsely chopped

2 carrots, chopped

6 cloves garlic, smashed and peeled

2 sprigs fresh rosemary or thyme (or ½ teaspoon dried thyme)

¼ teaspoon chili flakes (optional)

Large Parmesan rind

MANY HOME COOKS are stymied by dry beans. Well, that all changes today. After testing every variation I could find (soaked or not, baking soda or none, oven or slow cooker and so on) I can vouch for the ease and deliciousness of these beans.

Simmering pre-soaked beans gently in the oven with tons of aromatic vegetables makes the beans and their broth exceptionally delicious and versatile. Time is really the only requirement, so throw these on whenever you can and keep them stashed in the freezer.

I use a Parmesan rind in the broth here (that's the hard outer-edge of a chunk of fresh Parmesan—collect them and keep them in the freezer) but you can omit the rind for a fully vegan recipe.

Add some sausages to the beans and broth to make a stick-to-your-ribs dinner (perfect for a rainy weeknight), or mix them with tiny pasta shapes and tomato paste for a classic rustic Italian dish, or turn them into a vegetarian burrito filling.

To use the beans, thaw and reheat them gently. They're also tasty as a simple soup just drizzled with olive oil and served with crunchy toast.

1 Place the beans in a very large oven-proof pot or Dutch oven and cover with cold water by at least 5 inches. Stir in 1 teaspoon of the salt. Soak at room temperature for 6 to 24 hours.

2 Preheat the oven to 325°F. Drain the beans, then put them back into the pot and cover with water again, this time by 2 inches. Bring to a boil. Add the onion, celery, carrots, garlic, rosemary or thyme, chili flakes, Parmesan rind and the remaining 1½ teaspoons of salt. Return to a boil, then cover and transfer the pot to the oven. Bake 25 minutes, then taste one bean for tenderness and add more water if needed (it should cover the beans by an inch at all times). Continue to cook, checking on the beans every 5 to 10 minutes until they are tender without being mushy.

3 Cool completely, then package into 2- or 4-cup portions in freezer bags. Pat down the bags so they lie flat (this speeds up freezing and thawing) and freeze up to 3 months. To use, thaw in the fridge overnight, then gently reheat to a simmer.

Sausage and Bean Stew

Heat **1 tablespoon canola oil** in a large frying pan over high. Add **4 sausages** and cook about 4 minutes, or until they are golden on the bottom. Flip the sausages, reduce the heat to low and add **4 cups chopped kale**. Cover and cook 5 to 8 minutes, or until kale softens. Add **4 cups Brothy Beans** (thawed) and simmer gently, covered, until bubbly, about 10 minutes. Drizzle with **extra-virgin olive oil** and sprinkle with **shaved Parmesan**. SERVES 4.

Bean and Cheese Burritos

Combine **2 cups Brothy Beans** (thawed) with **¼ teaspoon smoked paprika** in a small pot and bring to a simmer. Purée with a potato masher or immersion blender and continue to cook until very thick. Stir in the **juice of 1 lime**. Layer in warm **tortillas** with **grated cheese**, **salsa**, **sliced avocado** and **hot sauce**. SERVES 2 TO 3.

Pasta Fagioli

Gently stir **4 cups Brothy Beans** (thawed) with a **156-mL can tomato paste** in a medium pot. Heat over medium until simmering gently, gently crushing the carrots, celery and garlic that's in the beans. In a separate pot, cook **1 cup small pasta** (such as ditalini) in boiling, salted water, until just tender. Drain, then add to the bean mixture and simmer for 1 minute. Serve drizzled with **extra-virgin olive oil** and **grated Parmesan**. SERVES 2 TO 3.

Big-Batch Whole Grains

PREP TIME 5 MINUTES | READY IN 30 MINUTES | MAKES ABOUT 10 SERVINGS

3 cups brown rice, wheat berries, farro, quinoa or barley

1 tablespoon salt

WHOLE GRAINS ARE delicious, versatile and healthy, but they take a long time to cook. Happily, once cooked they freeze beautifully, so years ago I started doubling every batch and freezing half. It's such a boon for my future rushed-weeknight self! I reheat these grains as an almost-instant side dish for stir-fries or as the base for the three recipes that follow.

Using this method, known as the pasta method for obvious reasons, is hands-down the easiest way to cook almost any grain. Simply simmer any grain in boiling, salted water until tender, then drain—no need to remember water-to-grain ratios. For smaller grains, like quinoa, you'll need a fine-mesh strainer so the batch doesn't go down the drain.

With cooked grains on hand, dinner ideas abound: think hearty fried rice, a refreshing salad packed with veggies or grain bowls topped with roasted and raw vegetables and a heavenly tahini dressing. To thaw and reheat, plunge the grains into boiling water and cook one minute.

1 Boil a very large pot of water. Add the rice and salt, stir, and return to boiling; then reduce heat and simmer gently (there should be lots of small bubbles on the surface) until the grains are tender, anywhere from 20 to 40 minutes. Try a few grains every 5 minutes after the 20-minute mark to check on their doneness.

2 Drain and transfer the grains to a large rimmed baking pan set on a cooling rack. Cool the grains completely, then package in 2-cup portions in freezer bags. Pat down the bags so they lie flat (this speeds up both freezing and thawing) and freeze up to 3 months.

Modern Fried Rice

Heat **2 tablespoons canola oil** in a large non-stick frying pan over medium high. Add **1 cup chopped broccoli** and **3 chopped green onions**. Cook 2 minutes. Add **1 cup edamame**, **3 minced cloves garlic** and **2 tablespoons chopped fresh ginger**. Cook 2 minutes. Add **2 cups Big-Batch Whole Grains** and cook, stirring often, until very hot. Make some space in the middle of the pan. Add **1 teaspoon toasted sesame oil**, then add **2 beaten eggs**. Cook 1 minute then stir the eggs into the grains and vegetables until well mixed. Stir in **1 to 2 tablespoons soy sauce**. SERVES 2.

Grain Bowls with Creamy Tahini Dressing

Whisk **½ cup tahini** with **2 tablespoons fresh lemon juice**, **2 teaspoons maple syrup**, **⅛ teaspoon garlic powder** and **⅛ teaspoon salt**. Whisk in **⅓ cup water**. Reserve. Reheat **2 cups Big-Batch Whole Grains** and divide between 2 bowls. Top with **sliced chicken**, **cubed roasted squash**, **sliced avocado**, **fresh arugula** and **crumbled feta**. Drizzle with **tahini dressing**. Sprinkle with **chopped toasted almonds** and **mint**. SERVES 2.

Vegetable Grain Salad

Whisk **2 tablespoons red wine vinegar** with **¼ teaspoon salt** and **¼ teaspoon sugar** in a large bowl. Whisk in **3 tablespoons extra-virgin olive oil**. Stir in **2 cups Big-Batch Whole Grains, 1 cup chopped cucumber, 1 cup halved cherry tomatoes, ½ cup chopped celery, ½ cup chopped fresh parsley** and **½ cup chopped pitted kalamata olives**. SERVES 2.

Easy Classic Bolognese

PREP TIME 30 MINUTES | **READY IN** ABOUT 90 MINUTES | **MAKES** ABOUT 12–15 SERVINGS

1 tablespoon butter

2 onions, finely chopped

4 stalks celery,
very finely chopped

2 carrots, very
finely chopped

1 kg lean ground beef

450 g ground
pork or veal

2 cups whole milk
(see Tip on facing page)

1½ cups dry white wine

2 156-mL cans
tomato paste

1½ teaspoons salt

Piece of fresh whole
nutmeg (optional)

SPAGHETTI BOLOGNESE WAS a staple of my early years. My mom made it by sautéing celery and onion, then adding ground beef, a big spoonful of dried oregano and several cans of whole tomatoes. Delicious, and we all loved it. However, it's not the official ragu from Bologna, and when I first tasted that dish in Italy, I pretty well fell off my chair. Traditional bolognese includes only a very little bit of tomato, certainly no oregano and lots of wine and milk (I know, milk?!).

It is, without hyperbole, outrageously delicious. After tasting it, I began to crave it and could accept no substitutes, so I made Bolognese myself. It's easy, but it does take some simmering time. Good thing it freezes like a charm—now I just make bigger and bigger batches.

Once the sauce is made, toss it with rigatoni, or use it for the most extraordinary lasagna. Looking for a noodle-free experience? Ladle the sauce over sweet roasted squash.

1 Melt the butter in a very large, wide, deep pot over medium high. Add the onion, celery and carrot and cook, stirring often, until the vegetables soften, about 7 minutes. Add the beef and pork and cook, stirring often, until the meat is halfway cooked, about 5 minutes.

2 Add the milk and bring to a boil (the mixture will look all wrong at this point but don't worry!). Simmer about 8 minutes, stirring to break the meat up into very small bits.

3 Whisk the wine and tomato paste together, then add to the pot along with the salt and about 10 gratings of nutmeg. Bring to a boil, then reduce the heat so the mixture simmers very gently (just a few bubbles popping on the surface every second). Simmer like this, stirring every now and then, for 1 hour, or until the sauce is deep red and very thick.

4 Cool completely, then package into 2-cup portions in freezer bags. Pat down the bags so they lie flat (this speeds up freezing and thawing) and freeze for up to 2 months. To use, thaw in the fridge overnight then gently reheat with a splash of water and bring to a simmer.

Rigatoni Bolognese

Cook **225 g rigatoni** in boiling, salted water until tender. Drain, reserving **1 cup of the cooking water**. Return the pasta to the pot along with **¼ cup butter**. Turn the heat to low and stir until the butter melts and coats the pasta. Add **2 cups Easy Classic Bolognese**, reheated, and ½ cup of the reserved cooking water. Stir until the pasta is coated with the sauce, adding a bit more reserved cooking water if needed. Serve sprinkled with **freshly grated Parmesan**. SERVES 2 TO 3.

Bolognese Squash Bowl

Cut **1 medium-sized round squash** (such as buttercup) into quarters. De-seed, then brush with **canola oil** and sprinkle with **salt**. Roast at 400°F on a parchment-lined baking pan for 35 to 45 minutes, or until tender. Gently heat **2 cups Easy Classic Bolognese** with **¼ cup white wine or water** until piping hot. Spoon over roasted squash. Top each one with about **3 table-spoons ricotta**. SERVES 4.

TIP It's important to use whole milk here, which tenderizes the meat and makes the sauce mysteriously creamy. Fresh nutmeg is also ideal for this recipe. Look for whole nutmegs in bulk stores or bigger super-markets, then grate them on a rasp as needed. If you can't find any fresh nutmeg, skip it.

My Ultimate Lasagna

PREP TIME 45 MINUTES | **READY IN** 1¾ HOURS | **SERVES** 9–12

¼ cup butter

¼ cup all-purpose flour

2½ cups milk

¼ teaspoon salt

Fresh nutmeg

12 lasagna noodles

5 cups Easy
Classic Bolognese
(see page 136)

2 cups grated mozzarella

½ cup grated Parmesan

I'M BAD AT CHOOSING favourites—I struggle to pin down a favourite band, dessert or movie—but when it comes to an all-time best-loved dish, this is it without question. The combination of luscious bolognese with layers of noodles and creamy béchamel—there's not even spinach or ricotta to interfere with this holy trinity!—is just total lasagna bliss. This recipe takes some time, but not much effort, and the end result is so superb you might give up frozen store-bought lasagna forever.

1 Make a béchamel: melt butter in a medium pot over medium. Whisk in flour and cook 1 minute, then gradually whisk in milk. Cook and whisk until thickened. Stir in salt and about 5 gratings of fresh nutmeg. Reserve.

2 Cook lasagna noodles in boiling salted water until barely tender. Drain, reserving 1 cup of cooking water. Rinse the noodles with cool water until cold.

3 Combine Easy Classic Bolognese with the reserved pasta water. Spread about ½ cup of the béchamel across the bottom of a 9×13-inch baking dish. Top with 3 noodles lengthwise (they will be too short for the dish, so just place them in the centre). Top with 1 more heaping cup of bolognese mixture. Top again with about ½ cup béchamel, then 3 noodles. Repeat the meat-béchamel-noodles layers, finishing with béchamel. Sprinkle with mozzarella. Cover with foil and bake at 350°F for 30 minutes.

4 Remove the foil and sprinkle with Parmesan. Bake 15 minutes, or until bubbling and golden here and there. Let stand at least 10 minutes before serving.

The Family Table

HAVING A FAMILY simultaneously draws us to the table and keeps us away. It's often parenthood that reminds us of the importance of regular dinners and inspires us to make them a priority. And when it works, it's amazing. My fondest childhood memories are of the five Tanseys tucking into dinner and conversation at our old wooden kitchen table.

But when it doesn't quite work, it's the worst. When a partner gives up carbs, or when a snarly teenager lectures adults about destructive farming practices, or when a little kid won't eat anything green, it's easy to dismiss dinner and let those ungrateful louts fend for themselves.

I call this frustrating state of affairs "being out of sync." When you can't get everyone at the table to agree to the same meal, it's certainly tempting to give up on the dream of a happy dinner ritual. At the time of writing this book, our son craves steak, pork or chicken, and won't eat anything "mixed up together"; Michael is training for a marathon and prefers complex carbs and lots of plants; and I'm testing 90 diverse recipes for a cookbook. We're totally out of sync.

There are a few solutions to being out of sync. You could make separate meals for everyone (or, better yet, allow them to make their own), become an expert Batcher (see page 64) and have the freezer stocked with meal options for everyone. Even if everyone is eating different things, maybe being together at the table is all that matters. It's not always about the food.

You could also insist on some trade-offs from all parties. I know that for me, for now, family dinner is worth some compromises.

Here are a few things that work for us. I'd love to hear what works for you.

1 Call a family meeting. We keep it upbeat, but talk about why we think family dinner is important. We all contribute ideas and create a list of meals that everyone likes (or at least that everyone can tolerate or customize to meet their wants). The goal here is twofold: to generate ideas and to get buy-in from everyone in the family.

2 **Share the load.** Whether it's an idea for one dinner, or helping to shop, prep or clear up, everyone contributes, and we switch tasks too. Since I'm usually the dinner-maker, I force myself to take a supporting role sometimes. Even Thomas pitches in, and so Michael and I happily eat his picks two nights a week.

3 **Be considerate without catering.** When dishes can be served deconstructed (like tacos) or customized (half the pizza has meat, half the chicken has a spice rub), do it.

4 **Set some dinner table rules.** Ours include no screens, no bathroom talk, no "yucks." We sit together and have conversation, and we always thank the cook. (And, yes, adults too!)

5 **Eating isn't a fight.** Our son, like many kids, learned early that food can be a power game. So we refuse to play. If Thomas won't eat something, our (mostly) calm reply is, "You don't have to eat it." If he is still hungry after 10 or 15 minutes of sitting politely at the table, he can make himself a piece of toast or a bowl of cereal.

6 **Enjoy each other.** The conversation doesn't need to be deep and meaningful. It's fine to just be together. Try to remember why you like each other—with time, and the help of great low-stress dinners, that will be easy.

Come join our *Dinner, Uncomplicated* community, where you'll find all kinds of helpful ideas to make the family table a happy place. Come on over to facebook.com/groups/ dinneruncomplicated.

WEEKENDS AND CELEBRATIONS

WHETHER IT'S A relaxed Saturday or a special weeknight, sometimes you've got a little extra time to invest in dinner. None of these recipes are outright complicated, but they do take a little extra time, even if that's just in sourcing the ingredients. And they're all just a little bit extra special so your birthday honoree or dinner guests will feel the love.

Brandied Apple Pork

PREP TIME 10 MINUTES | **READY IN** 20 MINUTES | **SERVES** 4

BRANDY, APPLE AND cream is a classic flavour trio used in French cuisine, and after one bite you'll know why. The combination is tart, sweet and rich—perfect for pork tenderloin, which can admittedly be a touch bland without a great sauce. To me, adding brandy to anything makes it worthy of company or any special meal. I serve this with Perfect Mashed Potatoes (page 176) to soak up the sauce and Buttery Mushrooms (page 172) for texture.

½ cup all-purpose flour

½ teaspoon dried thyme

½ teaspoon salt

675 g pork tenderloin

2 tablespoons butter

1 tablespoon canola oil

½ cup apple juice

¼ cup brandy

2 tablespoons 35% cream

½ teaspoon Dijon

1   Combine the flour, thyme and salt in a shallow bowl. Cut the pork into 8 equal-sized medallions.

2   Melt the butter with the oil in a large frying pan over medium high. While it's melting, dredge a piece of pork in the flour mixture. Shake off the excess, then place the piece cut-side-down into the pan, pressing gently on the pork with your fingers to flatten it slightly. Repeat with the remaining pork. Cook 2 to 3 minutes per side, or until golden. Transfer the pork to a plate.

3   Add the apple juice and brandy to the pan and increase the heat to high. Bring to a boil and cook, scraping up the brown bits from the bottom of the pan, for about 1 minute. Add the pork back to the pan and reduce the heat to medium. Cook, turning the pork over every now and then, 5 to 7 minutes, or until the pork is cooked through or an instant-read thermometer inserted into the centre of one piece reads 150°F. Transfer to a serving platter.

4   Add the cream and Dijon to the pan and whisk to combine. Cook about 1 minute, or until thickened slightly. Pour over the pork.

TIP   It's a myth that pork that looks pink is unsafe to eat. As long as it's cooked to 150°F, you're good to go, and the meat will be much juicier and more delicious than overcooked brown pork. The exception is ground pork, which, like all ground meats, should be cooked thoroughly.

Chicken Parmesan

PREP TIME 25 MINUTES | **READY IN** ABOUT 45 MINUTES | **SERVES** 6

3 boneless, skinless
chicken breasts

½ teaspoon salt

2 eggs

½ cup all-purpose flour

¾ cup plain fine
breadcrumbs

½ teaspoon oregano

¼ teaspoon
garlic powder

3 tablespoons canola oil,
plus more if needed

1½ cups plain
tomato sauce

1 cup shredded
mozzarella

2 tablespoons
grated Parmesan

MY FRIEND MARY made chicken Parmesan for us one recent evening. We all sat around her kitchen island chatting while Mary cooked and the kids played (that's my idea of perfect happiness, by the way). The meal was delicious comfort food at its finest, and it was the first time I'd had chicken Parmesan that wasn't greasy and heavy. Naturally, I begged for her recipe, since I'd never made it myself, and it has fast become one of our family's favourites.

Serve this with pasta, Creamy Polenta (page 173) or Perfect Mashed Potatoes (page 176) and a big green salad.

---

1 Carefully slice each chicken breast in half horizontally, starting at the thicker end. Place 2 pieces in a freezer bag. Use a mallet or a heavy frying pan to gently but firmly pound the meat evenly, until it's about ¼ inch thick. Remove the chicken to a plate and repeat with the remaining 4 pieces. Sprinkle the chicken all over with the salt.

2 Lightly beat the eggs in a wide, shallow bowl. Pour the flour and breadcrumbs into separate wide, shallow bowls. Stir the oregano and garlic powder into the breadcrumbs. Dip one chicken piece into the flour, coating it on all sides. Gently tap off the excess, then dip it into the egg mixture and let the excess drip off. Then, place the chicken in the breadcrumbs and coat it on all sides, pressing gently to make the crumbs stick. Gently tap off the excess, then place the breaded chicken on a baking sheet or large plate. Repeat with the remaining chicken.

3 Heat the oil in a large, wide frying pan over medium high. Once it's hot (it will shimmer a bit), carefully add 2 to 4 chicken pieces, making sure there is lots of space around each one. Cook about 2 minutes per side, or until deeply golden, then remove to the plate or baking sheet. Repeat with the remaining chicken, adding a bit more oil and reducing the heat as required.

4   Pour 1 cup of the tomato sauce into a 9×13-inch baking dish. Place the chicken over the sauce. Spoon a little of the extra tomato sauce over each chicken piece. Sprinkle with mozzarella and Parmesan. Bake 10 to 15 minutes, or until the sauce is bubbly.

TIP   You can use 6 chicken thighs in place of the breasts. Do not slice them, but pound them as the recipe instructs. They take about the same amount of cooking time.

Butter-Roasted Masala Fish

PREP TIME 10 MINUTES | **READY IN** 20 MINUTES | **SERVES** 4

I FIRST TASTED butter-roasted fish at a spice-blending workshop in Toronto. The teacher, a gregarious Indian woman, used lemon juice, butter and a blend of about 17 different spices on rich halibut fillets. It was out-of-this-world delicious. The rich, almost-creamy fish was a perfect match for the complex spice mix, and the method of using butter to carry both heat and flavour all over the delicate fish was new to me (and totally genius!).

Halibut and black cod are special-occasion ingredients in our house since they're fairly pricey, and they often need to be purchased from a fish store (preferably frozen to make sure the fish is as fresh as possible). But roasting the fish in butter makes it seem even more special, somehow. Serve this with basmati rice to soak up the luscious butter sauce and a green vegetable like Lemony Braised Leeks (page 176).

4 teaspoons lime juice

¼ teaspoon salt

2 tablespoons mild curry powder

¼ teaspoon garlic powder

¼ teaspoon ground ginger

¼ teaspoon onion powder

⅓ cup melted butter, divided

4 skinless black cod or halibut fillets (each about 115 g)

1 Preheat the oven to 425°F. Stir the lime juice and salt with the curry, garlic, ginger and onion powders together in a small bowl until smooth. Stir in 2 tablespoons of the butter. Pour the remaining butter in a very small baking dish, just big enough to fit all the fish.

2 Dry the fish fillets with paper towels and place them in the baking dish. Roll them around so all sides are coated in butter. Smear the spice mixture over the top and sides of each piece of fish. Roast 5 minutes, then spoon some of the butter in the pan over the fish. Roast another 5 to 7 minutes, or until a metal skewer poked into the middle of one piece of fish feels warm.

Rosemary Beef Stew

PREP TIME 35 MINUTES | **READY IN** ABOUT 3 HOURS | **SERVES** 6

3 tablespoons
canola oil, divided

1 kg beef stew meat

½ teaspoon salt, divided

3 large carrots, chopped
into bite-sized pieces

2 yellow onions, chopped

4 cloves garlic, minced

¼ cup all-purpose flour

1 L beef broth

1 sprig fresh rosemary

¾ cup frozen peas

1 cup all-purpose flour

2 teaspoons
baking powder

1 teaspoon chopped
fresh rosemary

¼ teaspoon salt

¾ cup milk

MY BELOVED AUNT ANN loved to cook—and eat! She had every important cookbook and used them to make all kinds of fancy dishes. When I was a teenager, she once taught me to make an elegant lamb stew with rosemary dumplings, plus a watercress salad with walnut dressing. It seemed like the height of sophistication to me.

After she became ill and had to be hospitalized, my mom, dad and I dismantled her home—a sad task made easier by sharing happy and funny memories each time we came across some treasure. In the kitchen drawers we found an old newspaper clipping, the source recipe for her lamb stew. It's a chic but warming dish that we now make often, especially on Ann's birthday to celebrate and remember her.

I adjust the original recipe a bit and use beef, which is easier to find, but if you can get lamb stew meat, feel free to use it instead! The dumplings are fun and tasty, but the stew is perfectly good without them too.

---

1 Preheat the oven to 300°F. Heat 2 tablespoons of the oil in a large, deep Dutch oven over medium high. Add about half of the beef (it should fit in a single layer) then sprinkle with about half of the salt. Cook 2 to 3 minutes, or until just the undersides have browned. Transfer the beef to a plate, then add the remaining beef and sprinkle with the remaining salt. Cook another 2 to 3 minutes, or until just the undersides have browned. Transfer to the plate.

2 Add the remaining 1 tablespoon of oil then add the carrots and onions. Cook, stirring often, 4 to 5 minutes, or until the vegetables start to soften. Add the garlic and cook another minute. Add the beef, then sprinkle evenly with the flour. Cook, stirring the flour into the mixture, about 1 minute. Add the broth and stir very well. Add the rosemary. Bring to a gentle boil, then cover and transfer to the oven. Bake 2½ hours, stirring once or twice.

3 Remove and discard the rosemary stem (the leaves will be in the stew). Stir in the peas. Serve immediately or add the dumplings (see optional next step).

4 For the rosemary dumplings, stir 1 cup all-purpose flour with the baking powder, chopped fresh rosemary and salt in a medium bowl. Stir in the milk. Drop into 6 large dollops over the simmering stew, then cover and bake another 15 minutes or until the dumplings are fluffy and cooked through.

Duck Breasts with Grapes

PREP TIME 10 MINUTES | **READY IN** 30 MINUTES | **SERVES** 4

HOLD ON—DON'T TURN the page! I promise you that duck is no more complicated to cook than chicken. In fact, it might even be easier. Duck is sophisticated and delicious, which makes it the perfect thing to impress anyone who needs impressing.

This is the very same technique as my Upside-Down Chicken with Preserved Lemon (page 86). Cooking the duck's skin very slowly allows the fat to melt, which crisps up the skin without overcooking the meat. A quick sweet and sour grape sauce is a great match. Duck breast is most tender and delicious when it is served medium rare or medium at most. I use kosher salt here because it's easier to rub into the skin; if you don't have any, use ½ teaspoon regular salt and sprinkle it over the skin (but not into the cuts).

Serve this with Perfect Mashed Potatoes (page 176) and Lemony Braised Leeks (page 176).

2 boneless duck breasts (each about 250 g)

1 teaspoon kosher salt

2 shallots, finely chopped

1 cup seedless red grapes, halved

¼ cup dry white vermouth

1 Dry the duck skin well with paper towels. Use a sharp knife to cut a criss-cross pattern into the skin of each breast. The lines should be about ¼-inch apart across the whole skin and should cut into the fat below the skin without cutting through to the meat. Sprinkle the skin with kosher salt and gently rub into the cuts.

2 Place the duck skin-side-down in a cold frying pan (preferably cast iron). Turn the heat on medium low and cook about 20 minutes without flipping or moving it until the skin is dark gold. As the fat accumulates in the pan, spoon it out into a bowl. Once the skin is deeply golden, flip the duck and cook another 5 minutes for medium rare (add 5 more minutes for medium). Transfer to a cutting board to rest for 5 to 15 minutes.

3 Drain the fat from the frying pan into a bowl, then add 2 table-spoons back into the pan. Add the shallots and cook 3 minutes or until softened. Add the grapes and cook 2 minutes or until they soften and start to release their juice. Add the vermouth and cook 1 minute or until just slightly thickened. Carve the duck into ¼-inch slices. Spoon the sauce overtop.

Kale and Feta Spanakopita Pie

PREP TIME 35 MINUTES | **READY IN** 75 MINUTES | **SERVES** 6 TO 8

285-g bag chopped kale

300-g package frozen
leaf spinach, thawed

250 g cream cheese,
at room temperature

2 eggs

4 green onions,
finely chopped

¼ cup chopped
fresh parsley

½ teaspoon salt

1 cup crumbled feta

4 sheets phyllo
pastry (thawed—
see Tip on facing page)

¼ cup butter, melted

I OFTEN GET asked about vegetarian party dishes. Whether it's a big family Christmas dinner or a neighbourhood potluck, a special vegetarian entrée isn't just a welcome addition anymore—it's often required! Whatever the occasion, this is your new go-to dish, because, truly, it's unforgettable.

If you're a phyllo novice, don't fret. It looks terribly fussy but it's really very forgiving. You can stack it, crease it and rip it, but as long as you brush it with enough butter, it will end up crisp, golden and delicious. If making this recipe for a party, you might consider making two, since you'll have the phyllo thawed anyways. It will be gobbled up by vegetarians and meat eaters alike, and it's even fabulous heated up the next day.

MAKE IT AHEAD The filling can be mixed and kept in the fridge for up to 24 hours.

1 Preheat the oven to 400°F. Place the kale in a large pot. Add several spoonfuls of water, cover and bring to a boil. Reduce the heat and let the kale cook gently, until it is very soft, about 5 minutes. Drain in a colander then rinse with cold water. Add the spinach to the colander, then squeeze as much liquid as possible from the greens (squeeze handfuls of the mixture as hard as you can).

2 Chop the greens finely. Combine them with the cream cheese, eggs, onions, parsley and salt in a large bowl and stir very well until combined (you can do this with an electric mixer if you prefer). Stir in the feta. Reserve.

3 Place one sheet of phyllo on the counter, then brush it with butter using a natural bristle brush, covering the entire surface lightly. Take another sheet of phyllo and place it on top of the first sheet, rotating the top sheet 90 degrees so it's perpendicular to the bottom sheet. Brush the phyllo with butter. Place a third sheet crosswise over the first two and brush with butter, then add a fourth sheet of phyllo perpendicular to the third sheet. Brush the top with butter.

4 Brush a 9-inch pie dish with butter. Transfer the buttered phyllo to the pie dish, tucking it into the corners and letting the extra hang over the sides. Add the kale mixture and smooth into an even layer. Fold the overhanging phyllo loosely over the spinach mixture. Brush the top with the remaining butter. Bake 35 to 40 minutes, or until the phyllo is deeply golden all over. Let stand 10 minutes before slicing.

TIP To use phyllo pastry, first thaw it in the package, either overnight in the fridge or on the counter for an hour or two. Unroll the package of phyllo and unfold it so all the sheets are in a single layer. Transfer one whole sheet to the counter to brush with butter as above, and cover the remaining stack of phyllo with a slightly damp tea towel. Once you've used what you need, reroll the phyllo, wrap it very well with plastic wrap and keep it in the fridge for up to a week.

Baked Shells with Spinach and Ricotta

PREP TIME 25 MINUTES | **READY IN** ABOUT 1 HOUR | **SERVES** 6 TO 8

34 jumbo pasta
shells (about 450 g)

3 tablespoons
butter, divided

1 onion, finely chopped

¼ tsp salt

3 cloves garlic, minced

300-g package frozen
leaf spinach, thawed

2 cups ricotta
(about 425 g)

Fresh nutmeg (optional)

2 cups marinara sauce

2 cups shredded
mozzarella

½ cup Parmesan

ANY COMBINATION OF spinach and ricotta is a hit with me. Stuff it into tortellini, calzones, even an omelette and I'll dig in with delight. But this rendition is my favourite. There's just enough pasta and tons of my beloved spinach and ricotta, all buried under marinara and melty cheese. I've been known to take this to a potluck and then eat much of it myself (sorry, friends!).

I prefer to use frozen spinach in this recipe, not only because it's faster but also because I can squeeze more moisture out of thawed spinach, and getting rid of as much moisture as possible is important to making sure the overall dish isn't soggy.

MAKE IT AHEAD The filling can be made and the pasta cooked and cooled up to 24 hours ahead. Assemble and bake just before serving.

1 Boil the pasta in a large pot of boiling well salted water for 7 minutes, or until barely tender (the shells will continue to cook in the oven). Drain and rinse until cold. Brush a 9×13-inch baking dish with 1 tablespoon of the butter. Add the shells to the dish.

2 Melt the remaining butter in a large frying pan over medium. Add the onion and salt and cook, stirring occasionally, until the onions are translucent and very soft, about 5 minutes. Add the garlic and cook another 1 minute. Squeeze as much liquid out of the spinach as possible, then add it to the pan. Cook about 1 minute. Remove from heat. Stir in the ricotta and about 5 gratings of nutmeg. Transfer this mixture to a large plastic freezer bag. Snip off one corner of the bag, creating a hole about 1 inch wide.

3 Squeeze the filling into each shell, until almost full, then replace each one open-side-up. Spoon the marinara sauce over the shells. Sprinkle with mozzarella. Bake 20 minutes, or until the cheese is melted and a little bubbly. Sprinkle with Parmesan, then turn on the broiler to high and broil 2 to 3 minutes, or until browned in places.

Golden Seared Scallops

PREP TIME 5 MINUTES | **READY IN** 20 MINUTES | **SERVES** 3 TO 4

WHEN I SEE scallops on the menu of a classy restaurant, I always order them. Restaurants do such a brilliant job of cooking scallops so they are deeply golden, beautifully tender and full of flavour. To replicate them at home, the most important step—and the one that takes the most time—is finding the right scallops. Most supermarket scallops are brined (that is, chemically treated to retain moisture) so they never sear properly, no matter how you cook them. They end up spongy or rubbery, and always pale beige. For glorious, crusty-edged, golden, tender restaurant-style scallops you need dry scallops.

So how do you find dry scallops? You'll almost certainly need to go to a fish shop to buy them. Dry scallops are slightly translucent, while wet scallops are all opaque and milky-white. Dry scallops will also be pricier than wet (since you're buying all scallop and not a combination of scallop and brine). I prefer to buy mine vacuum-sealed and frozen to ensure maximum freshness. They'll still be damp (that's the nature of shellfish) but they won't release a puddle of liquid in the frying pan.

These make a spectacular meal for a date night in or very small dinner party. Serve with Creamy Polenta (page 173) and Buttery Mushrooms (page 172).

625 g dry sea scallops

1 teaspoon kosher salt

2 tablespoons canola oil

Black pepper

---

1   Pat the scallops dry with paper towels. Place the scallops on a fresh layer of paper towels on a plate and sprinkle both sides with the salt. Let stand in the fridge for 15 minutes.

2   Heat the oil in a large cast iron frying pan over high for 1 to 2 minutes. Add the scallops, leaving space between each one. They should sizzle when they hit the pan. If they don't, remove them and wait until the pan is hotter. Cook about 2 minutes, or until the undersides of the scallops are dark gold, then carefully flip and cook another 30 seconds to 1 minute. Transfer to a fresh sheet of paper towel, then serve immediately, seasoned with freshly ground black pepper.

Mushroom and Gorgonzola Polenta Pie

PREP TIME 40 MINUTES | **READY IN** 1 HOUR | **SERVES** 6

10 very large white or brown mushrooms

2 tablespoons canola oil

1 teaspoon salt, divided

2 tablespoons butter

1 small onion, minced

225 g fresh spinach, chopped

5 cups water

1¼ cups fine cornmeal

¼ cup 35% cream

85 g semi-soft blue cheese, such as Gorgonzola

SOMETIMES I GET the best ideas in the grocery store. One day, while wandering through the produce section, wondering what to make for a vegetarian dinner party, I noticed that the white mushrooms on display were extraordinarily large. Usually they're about an inch across, but these were about three inches (don't you just love nature?). This dish immediately took shape in my brain. I picked up a bag of spinach and a package of cornmeal, knowing there was a neglected hunk of Gorgonzola in the fridge.

This naturally gluten-free vegetarian dish is superb as the centre-piece of a dinner party, or as the co-star (say, with a turkey or ham) of a family celebration. The combination of blue cheese with mushrooms is heavenly, but if you're staunchly anti-blue, feel free to use goat cheese or feta.

MAKE IT AHEAD Assemble the pie and keep chilled for up to 6 hours. When ready to cook, remove from the fridge and add about 15 minutes to the baking time.

---

1 Preheat the oven to 375°F. Wash the mushrooms and pat them dry, then gentry pry out the stems and reserve. Combine the mushroom caps with the oil and ¼ teaspoon salt in a 9×13-inch baking dish. Turn the mushrooms so they are stem-side-down. Roast 25 to 35 minutes, or until tender but not mushy.

2 Meanwhile, finely chop the mushroom stems. Melt the butter in a large non-stick frying pan. Add the onion and cook, stirring occasionally, 3 minutes or until onion is softened and butter is bubbly. Add the chopped stems and ¼ teaspoon salt and cook another three minutes. Add a few handfuls of spinach and cook, stirring often, until wilted. Add the rest of the spinach and cook until it wilts completely and there is very little moisture left in the pan. Reserve.

3 Boil the water in a medium pot, then reduce the heat to low and sprinkle in the cornmeal gradually, whisking constantly. Switch to a heat-proof spatula and cook, stirring constantly, until the mixture becomes thick, 4 to 8 minutes. Remove from heat and stir in the cream and ½ teaspoon salt. Stir in the spinach mixture.

4 Take the mushroom caps out of the baking dish and pour in the polenta mixture. Smooth it into an even layer. Place the mushroom caps on top. Crumble the cheese over everything. Bake 10 minutes or until the edges are bubbly. You can briefly broil the casserole if you like the top a bit more golden and crisp.

TIP Cornmeal comes in different sizes, from powdery-fine to chunky. Look for "fine" cornmeal, which has the texture of granulated sugar.

Sun-Dried Tomato and Chèvre Chicken

PREP TIME 15 MINUTES | **READY IN** 45 MINUTES | **SERVES** 6

IN THE MID-1990S, goat cheese and sun-dried tomatoes could do no wrong, especially when they were mixed together. Over the decade and various restaurant jobs I had, I stuffed that same blend into phyllo packets, ravioli and pork roasts, and even served it as a fancy vegetarian pâté. Fast-forward a few decades and those ingredients have gone out of food fashion, but that doesn't mean they're any less delicious. The creaminess of the cheese with the mellow punch of the tomatoes really gussies up plain chicken breasts.

This is a great dish for a dinner party, since it can be assembled in advance and baked when company arrives. Serve with Lemony Braised Leeks (page 176) and Crispy Oven Fries (page 174).

MAKE IT AHEAD Stuff the chicken and top with the breadcrumb mixture. Keep refrigerated for up to 4 hours. Add about 5 minutes to the baking time.

---

1 Preheat the oven to 400°F. Line a large rimmed baking pan with parchment. Mash the goat cheese, tomatoes, thyme, garlic powder and ¼ teaspoon of the salt together in a small bowl.

2 Slice a long, deep pocket into the fattest part of each chicken breast using a sharp paring knife. Spoon about 2 tablespoons of the goat cheese mixture into each pocket. (Force the stuffing deep into the pocket, but make sure the edges of the chicken still meet.) Transfer the chicken to the prepared baking pan and sprinkle with the remaining ¼ teaspoon of salt.

3 Stir the panko and butter together until well combined, then press onto the tops of each chicken breast. Bake 20 to 25 minutes, or until the topping is golden and the chicken's juices run clear. Let stand 5 minutes before serving.

113-g package
soft goat cheese

⅓ cup finely
chopped oil-packed
sun-dried tomatoes

2 teaspoons chopped
fresh thyme
(or 1 teaspoon dried)

¼ teaspoon
garlic powder

½ teaspoon salt, divided

6 small boneless,
skinless chicken breasts

⅓ cup panko

3 tablespoons
melted butter

Leek and Feta Quiche in a Potato Crust

PREP TIME 30 MINUTES | **READY IN** 75 MINUTES | **SERVES** 6

600 g Russet potatoes (about 2 medium to large)

¼ teaspoon salt

1 egg white (add the yolk to the filling)

2 teaspoons canola oil, divided

---

2 tablespoons butter

2 thin leeks, sliced into thin half moons (about 3 cups)

4 eggs, plus leftover yolk

1 cup milk

1 cup crumbled feta

¼ cup chopped fresh parsley

¼ teaspoon salt

ONE OF MY FIRST full-time cooking jobs was in the kitchen at a gourmet takeaway store—the kind where you can buy a slice of quiche for your lunch or two whole quiches for a party. I made many, many quiches at that job, and I was constantly trying new combinations for the filling. I forget how I landed on leeks and feta, but once I did it immediately became a personal—and customer—favourite. Around the same time a close friend was diagnosed with celiac disease, and I was so quiche-obsessed that I was determined to make them gluten-free. This grated potato crust was a delicious solution. The combination here, particularly with the hash-brownish crust, also lends itself perfectly to brunch.

1   Preheat the oven to 400°F. Peel the potatoes, then grate them (potatoes may brown; they will measure about 4 cups). Combine the potato and salt in a colander. Let drain in the sink or over a bowl for 10 minutes. Whisk the egg white in a medium bowl until frothy. Squeeze out as much liquid as you can from the potatoes, then add them to the egg white and stir well. Spray or brush a 9-inch pie dish with 1 teaspoon of the oil. Add the potato mixture and shape it into a crust shape, firmly pressing it into the base and up the sides of the dish. Tuck in any single potato strands so they do not burn. Bake 20 minutes, then brush all over with the remaining teaspoon of canola oil and bake another 10 to 15 minutes or until pale golden across the base. Reduce the oven to 350°F.

2   Melt the butter in a frying pan over medium. Add the leeks and cook, stirring often, 5 minutes, or until the leeks are softened. Whisk the eggs in a large bowl, adding the yolk left over from the crust, until well combined. Whisk in the milk, then stir in the feta, parsley, salt and leeks. Pour this mixture into the cooked crust (it's fine it the crust is still hot). Bake 25 to 35 minutes or until a knife inserted into the centre comes out clean. Let stand 10 minutes before serving.

TIP Leeks can hide dirt within their layers. The best way to clean them is to trim off the root end and the darker green tops. Slice each leek lengthwise. Wash the halves under cold running water, gently separating the layers to let the water run through them. Shake dry before chopping. Use only the white and pale green parts of the leek. Either discard or save green tops for stock.

Crispy Chicken with Spicy Black Bean Rice

PREP TIME 20 MINUTES | **READY IN** ABOUT 50 MINUTES | **SERVES** 4

THIS IS A FABULOUS cast iron pan dinner. Rice and black beans form the base and soak up all the flavours of the dish and the chicken, perched on top, gets crispy while staying very juicy. I like to bring the whole pan to the table for serving, for additional flourish.

The beans make this dish hearty enough to serve four, but if you're feeding big appetites feel free to roast some more chicken thighs on a separate pan (brush with oil and sprinkle with salt and pepper first).

---

1 Preheat the oven to 375°F. Heat a 10- or 12-inch oven-safe frying pan over high (cast iron is perfect here). Sprinkle about ¼ teaspoon of the salt over the skin of the chicken. Add the oil to the pan, then add the chicken skin-side-down and cook, without touching it, for about 3 minutes, or until the skin is golden. Transfer to a plate and reduce the heat to medium low.

2 Add the onions and green peppers and cook, stirring occasionally, for about 2 minutes, or until they start to soften. Stir in the garlic, jalapeno, cumin and the remaining salt and cook about 1 minute. Stir in the beans and broth, increase the heat to high and bring to a boil. Once it boils, turn off the heat and sprinkle the rice on top. Smooth the rice so it's submerged but don't stir it—if the rice ends up on the bottom of the pan, it might burn. Place the chicken skin-side-up over the rice.

3 Carefully transfer the pan to the oven and bake 30 to 35 minutes, or until the rice is tender and the chicken is golden and fully cooked. Let stand 5 minutes before serving.

1 teaspoon salt, divided

4 bone-in, skin-on chicken thighs

1 tablespoon canola oil

1 medium onion, finely chopped

1 small green pepper, diced

2 cloves garlic, minced

1 jalapeno, minced

2 teaspoons ground cumin

540-mL can black beans, rinsed

2 cups chicken broth

¾ cup basmati rice

My Kitchen Essentials

IT DOESN'T TAKE a ton of ingredients or special equipment to get your kitchen in fighting shape. Here are the basics I keep on hand at all times, as well as my most-useful pieces of gear and some of my favourite tricks and tips. With these tools and food staples, you can pull a delicious dinner out of thin air.

Ten Easy Meal Staples to Keep on Hand

1 Pasta or rice
2 Parmesan or feta cheese
3 Canned beans or chickpeas
4 Frozen peas or corn
5 Garlic
6 Onions
7 35% cream
8 Cheddar
9 Canned tomatoes or tomato paste
10 Dry white vermouth

Runner-up: Bread, soft tortillas or naan

Nine Multi-Purpose Kitchen Workhorses

1 Cast iron frying pan (about 10 inches)
2 Two rimmed baking pans (also called half sheet pans)
3 Sturdy box grater
4 Parchment paper
5 Non-stick frying pan
6 Cutting board
7 Three basic knives: a chef's knife, a paring knife, a serrated bread knife
8 Dutch oven
9 Blender (immersion or otherwise)

Runners-up: Digital scale, electric slow cooker

Eight Essential Spices

1 Cumin
2 Chili powder
3 Curry powder
4 Garlic powder
5 Cinnamon
6 Thyme
7 Chili flakes
8 Smoked paprika

Runner-up: Whole black peppercorns, if you like pepper on everything

Seven Splurge-Worthy Ingredients That Really Make a Difference to Flavour

1. Balsamic vinegar (spend closer to $20 than $2)
2. Extra-virgin olive oil (as above!)
3. Whole pieces of Parmesan
4. Oil-packed tuna
5. Meat from a good butcher
6. Responsibly sourced fish
7. Fresh lemons and limes

   Runner-up: Pure vanilla extract

Six Useful Gadgets Under $20

1. Rasp-style fine grater
2. A vegetable peeler (just remember— they get dull and need to be replaced!)
3. Garlic press
4. Kitchen scissors
5. Lemon juicer
6. Knife sharpener

   Runner-up: A bench scraper (sometimes called a pastry scraper)

Five Grocery Shortcuts That Aren't Worth It

1. Bottled lemon juice
2. Pre-chopped garlic
3. Pre-marinated meat
4. Frozen herbs
5. Pre-grated Parmesan

Four Grocery Shortcuts That Are Worth It

1. Frozen peas and corn
2. Marinara sauce
3. Shredded cheese when you're making something big, like lasagna
4. Rotisserie chicken

Three Ways to Fix a Dish That Needs a Flavour Boost

1. Add a squeeze of fresh lemon juice
2. Add a lump of butter or a drizzle of cream
3. Add salt

SIDE DISHES

MY GOLD STANDARD side dishes are quick, simple and versatile. Here is a collection of my favourites—all easy recipes that are designed to match with all kinds of different main courses.

Brussels Sprouts with Bacon

Cook **4 slices of bacon** until crispy. Drain, reserving the bacon and the fat separately. Trim the stem and outer leaves from **1 kg Brussels sprouts**. Cut each one in half lengthwise. Combine with about 3 tablespoons of the reserved bacon fat and toss well to coat. Preheat the oven to 450°F, then place a large, empty foil-lined baking pan in the oven for 4 minutes to heat. Carefully spread the sprouts on the hot pan in a single layer and sprinkle with **¼ teaspoon salt**. Roast 4 minutes, then flip the sprouts and roast another 3 to 5 minutes or until tender-crisp. Crumble the bacon overtop and drizzle with a little **balsamic vinegar**. SERVES 4 TO 6.

Buttery Mushrooms

Cut **450 g white or brown mushrooms** in half (or in quarters if they're quite large). Heat **1 tablespoon canola oil** in a very large, non-stick frying pan over high. Add the mushrooms and **1 garlic clove**, peeled and cut in half, and cook without stirring at all for 3 minutes, or until the undersides of the mushrooms are lightly golden. Add **¼ teaspoon salt**, then stir the mushrooms and cook another 3 minutes without stirring. Continue to cook, stirring occasionally, another 2 to 4 minutes or until the mushrooms are tender but not soft. Remove from heat and add **2 tablespoons butter**. Stir until the butter melts. Discard the garlic. Season with **chopped fresh parsley or thyme** and **freshly ground black pepper**. SERVES 3 TO 4.

Crunchy Coleslaw

Stir **⅓ cup mayonnaise** with **⅓ cup plain yogurt**, **2 teaspoons red wine vinegar**, **¼ teaspoon curry powder** and **¼ teaspoon salt** in a large bowl. Add **5 to 6 cups napa or Savoy cabbage**, very thinly sliced, **2 to 3 minced green onions** and **1 grated apple**. Stir very well to combine. Add **½ cup chopped fresh dill or parsley** and season well with **freshly ground black pepper**. SERVES 6 TO 8.

Creamy Polenta

Boil **6 cups of water** in a medium pot. Once it boils, reduce the heat to low and gradually whisk in **1¼ cups of fine cornmeal** and **¾ teaspoon salt**. Switch to a heat-proof spatula and cook, stirring often, until the polenta thickens, 6 to 8 minutes. Remove from heat and let stand 5 minutes. Stir in **¼ cup 35% cream or grated Parmesan** (or both!) and season with **freshly ground black pepper**. SERVES 4 TO 6.

Crispy Oven Fries

Peel **4 Russet potatoes**, then slice into ½-inch sticks. Divide the potatoes between 2 large rimmed baking pans lined with parchment. Drizzle each pan of potatoes with **1 tablespoon canola oil**. Toss well, then spread into a single layer. Sprinkle each pan with **¼ teaspoon salt**. Roast 10 minutes, then stir the potatoes and rotate the pans on the oven racks. Roast another 10 to 15 minutes, or until the potatoes are golden at the edges. SERVES 3 TO 4.

Flaky Biscuits

Combine **1 cup all-purpose flour, 1 cup whole-wheat flour, 4 teaspoons baking powder** and **½ teaspoon salt** in a large bowl. Add **1⅓ cups cold 35% cream** and stir well to combine. Transfer to a lightly floured counter and knead 3 or 4 times into a ball. Roll to about a 1-inch-thick circle. Use a 3-inch round cookie cutter (or an overturned drinking glass) to cut out 6 to 8 rounds. Transfer to a parchment-lined baking pan. Smush any scraps into the cookie cutter and force them into a round, then transfer that biscuit (my favourite one, by the way!) to the baking pan. Bake at 425°F for 12 to 15 minutes, or until dark golden on the bottoms and light golden on top. SERVES 6.

Garlicky Green Beans

Cook **350 g trimmed green beans** in a large pot of boiling, well salted water for 3 to 5 minutes, or until bright green and barely tender. (The beans should be very crisp still.) Immediately drain the beans and plunge them into a large bowl of ice water. Once the beans are fully cold, drain again. The beans can be made up to this point and kept in the fridge for up to 6 hours. Melt **2 tablespoons butter** in a large, non-stick frying pan over medium low. Add **1 large minced garlic clove** and cook 2 to 3 minutes, or until fragrant and butter is bubbling gently. Add the beans and cook, stirring, 2 to 4 minutes, or until piping hot. Sprinkle with **⅛ teaspoon salt**. SERVES 4.

Golden Cauliflower with Tahini Sauce

Chop **1 medium cauliflower** into small florets. Toss with **2 tablespoons canola oil** and **¼ teaspoon salt**. Spread in a single layer on a parchment-lined baking pan and roast at 425°F for 15 minutes, stirring once, or until deeply golden. Meanwhile stir **2 tablespoons tahini** with **1 very small minced garlic clove**, **4 teaspoons lemon juice** and **⅛ teaspoon salt** in a small bowl until smooth. Add **3 to 5 tablespoons cold water** and mix until it's the texture of ketchup. Drizzle over the cooked cauliflower. Garnish with a **pinch of ground cumin** and **chopped fresh parsley**. SERVES 4.

Lemony Braised Leeks

Heat **2 tablespoons butter** in a large, wide frying pan or pot over medium low. Add **3 large leeks**, trimmed and cut into ¼-inch half moons. Cover and cook, stirring occasionally, 7 to 10 minutes, or until tender and translucent. Add **½ cup chicken broth** and **2 tablespoons lemon juice** and cook another minute. Season with **freshly ground black pepper.** SERVES 3 TO 4.

Perfect Mashed Potatoes

Peel **8 medium or large Yukon Gold potatoes**, then cut each one in half and place in a large pot. Cover with lots of cold water and season with about **1 teaspoon salt**. Bring to a boil, then reduce the heat, cover and simmer 20 minutes or until very tender. Pass each potato through a ricer and into a large mixing bowl. Mix in **¼ cup room-temperature butter** and **¼ cup milk or cream**, then taste for salt. Transfer to a warmed serving bowl. Potatoes can be made ahead and kept chilled up to 12 hours. Reheat in a microwave on high at 1 minute intervals, stirring often, until piping hot. SERVES 4 TO 6.

Roasted Miso Eggplant

Slice **4 Japanese eggplant** in half lengthwise. Brush cut sides with **2 tablespoons canola oil** and sprinkle with **¼ teaspoon salt**. Place cut-side-down on a parchment-lined baking pan. Roast at 400°F for 20 minutes, then carefully flip and drizzle with **1 more tablespoon canola oil**. Roast another 5 to 10 minutes, or until light golden and very tender. Meanwhile stir **2 tablespoons miso** with **1 teaspoon honey**, **1 teaspoon rice vinegar** and **1 teaspoon grated fresh ginger**. Spread this mixture over the cut-side of the roasted eggplant. Roast another 5 minutes, or until miso mixture is bubbly. SERVES 4.

Hot Honeyed Sweet Potatoes

Chop **3 to 4 large sweet potatoes** (peeled if you prefer) into 1-inch slices. Toss with **2 tablespoons canola oil** and **¼ teaspoon salt** on a large parchment-lined baking pan. Roast at 400°F for 20 to 25 minutes, flipping halfway, or until golden and tender. Meanwhile whisk **3 tablespoons melted butter** with **1 tablespoon each honey and Tabasco**. Spoon over the roasted potatoes. SERVES 4.

GOLD STARS

IT'S THE GREATEST privilege of my life to be welcomed into your kitchens and your lives by way of these recipes. Thank you for reading and using this book.

Bruce Sellery has been a friend and cheerleader for years, and it was his suggestion to call Jesse Finkelstein at Page Two Books. That phone call reset my vision for what my life as an author could be. I'm deeply grateful to Bruce as well as to Jesse and the team at Page Two, who have been fierce champions of me and this book from the word go.

It is always such a joy to be in a photo studio with photographers Suech and Beck, food stylist Lindsay Guscott and prop stylist Emily Howes. They are talented artists, and they love these recipes as much as I do. Their creativity made the dishes come to life. We also couldn't have managed it so well without the able hands of Leah Wildman.

The *Dinner, Uncomplicated* community tested every recipe in this book (multiple times over) and provided priceless feedback to make the recipes easier, clearer and more delicious. You guys rock.

Support, great ideas and occasional stern lectures came from Sarah Casey, Bruce Cooper, Lian Dolan and the Satellite Sisterhood, Matt Dupuis, Karyn Gordon, Michelle Hillier, Stacy Irvine, Jenny Kingsley, Adrian Lyons, Chris Nuttall-Smith, Michelle Pennock, Greta Podleski, Jane Proctor, Heather Trim, Julie Van Rosendaal and Leanne Webb. Shannon Moroney gets a special extra star for being not just a great friend but also a therapist and singing partner. Thanks also to my splendid work families at *Cityline*, CBC Radio and George Brown College.

Huge thanks to Donna and Sue at Miik for outfitting me with sustainable, beautiful and insanely comfortable clothes for all my media appearances and for this book.

My family is always ready to dole out advice and a stiff cocktail as required. Thanks in particular to my brother Dylan, who encouraged me to self-publish, and my sister Erin, who was excited for the book even before I could be. My extraordinary parents, Margaret and Brian, have always believed I could do anything, and taught me the downright joy of the daily dinner ritual. I always feel lucky to be their daughter.

My editor Katie Dupuis conveniently is also my best friend (so texting her 27 times a day isn't cause for concern). She saw my vision for this book better than I could, and shaped my impassioned ramblings with the gentlest touch. I'm so proud of our second book.

Michael and Thomas happily ate dinner from a buffet of "test kitchen scraps" for months while I was working on these recipes. Thomas gives the coziest hugs, has the best palate in the family and never hesitates to tell me if he's not thrilled by one of my creations (and even better, if he is!). Michael steadfastly supports and encourages me and only occasionally insists on taking a break and having roast chicken. Sharing dinner is the best part of my day, every day, and there's no place I'd rather be.

Thank you.

INDEX

My husband and I could never agree on what to eat until Claire and her amazing ideas became part of our everyday life. Now I only have to say, "It's from Claire's book," and everyone knows it is going to be great.

ANNE

The Grain Bowls with Creamy Tahini Dressing are *amazing*. We make them weekly, and my kids want to drink the leftover dressing. Delicious!

KRISTEN

Claire's recipes and the stories that accompany them are delightful and inspiring, and the meals turn out perfectly every time. We often give Claire's books as gifts, and our friends and family love her down-to-earth style and easy-to-find ingredients—including my mother-in-law, who is a retired Home Ec teacher and cooks gourmet meals even at the cottage.

PATTI

My whole family loved the Mushroom and Lentil Ragu. My boys thought they could taste ground beef in it, and the crunchy topping is such a genius idea. So great to have vegan recipes included!

JESSICA

Claire's recipes make our weeknight cooking so fun and easy. They use simple ingredients, and the whole family can find something they love. Our 9- and 12-year-old daughters are excited to make *us* meals now—and not just chocolate chip cookies! Does it get any better than that?

DAVE

The Creamy Chicken and Vegetable Pot Pie is so, so, so good. There were clean plates all around and very little talking while my family was eating. Definitely a hit!

LORRAINE

The Coconut Chicken Curry is awwwwesome. I asked my mom to put the leftovers in my lunchbox.

JAMES, AGE 8

We use *Uncomplicated* so much in our house that the kids assume anything yummy is from the book—and 99 percent of the time, they're right! Whenever we eat something delicious, someone will put their fork down and say, "Oh, Claire."

CAROL

Uncomplicated truly changed my life. Before I was given this book, I was intimidated by cooking and didn't even know where to begin. But the recipes are so easy to understand, and with each meal I gained the confidence to try more. I've now been dubbed "the best chef in the family."

CANDACE

It's shocking how often we opted for takeout before we got *Uncomplicated*. It's been a life changer, and now we're having beautiful home-cooked meals every day with barely any effort. It feels good to feel good about what we're eating, and even better to see the difference on our wallets and waistlines. I don't even miss takeout!

JEFF